Doing Business in India

&

Understanding Pitfalls

By

Subodh Gupta

Corporate Trainer

First Edition July 2008

Copy Editor: Mahnaz Khan

ISBN 978-0-9556882-7-0

Published by
Subodh Gupta
+44(0)7966275913
Head office: London (UK)
Email: info@subodhgupta.co.uk
www.subodhgupta.co.uk

This book is available for special discounts on bulk purchases. Please contact at the publisher email address or phone number.

Publisher Note:

The reader should not regard this book as a substitute advice for a qualified legal or other professional advice. The views expressed in this book are of the author based on his personal experience while living in India and Great Britain and may not be suitable for every situation. Neither the publisher nor the author shall be liable for any damages arising here from.

Acknowledgements

I am grateful to my parents and all my teachers who taught me at various stages of my life & shared with me their wisdom.

I am also thankful to the copy editor Mahnaz Khan for taking time out from her busy schedule to help me to complete my book.

Content

Introduction:

This book is about understanding various pitfalls while doing business in India.

India offers many opportunities for those who are brave enough to take risk and smart enough to avoid the pitfalls.

This practical book will create awareness about business environment in India and certainly help you in avoiding the cost of expensive mistakes.

This book is written by an Indian entrepreneur for Westerners who are doing business with Indians or are planning to do business in India.

The word Westerner or Western used in this book refers to people from the UK, Europe, Canada, Australia and US.

Most organization corporate executives are making their business calculations about Indian domestic market based on numbers i.e. 300 million middle class Indians and this book is written focussing on that *assumed* middle class Income group Indians though basic concept applies to others income groups as well.

Doing business in India requires a variety of new skills and sets of knowledge in comparison to that needed in the Western countries in order to be successful. The working culture and day to day management style are very different from the Western style which further leads to confusion.

Having worked for approximately 12 years in India as an entrepreneur, a guest professor to various MBA schools, a training consultant for The Times of India Group and 3 years in the UK, I can see various pitfalls which a Western businessman or a Western company would experience in India if they do not prepare in advance.

The purpose of this book is not to scare you but to make you more aware so you can take better & well informed decisions while doing business in India.

The book is divided into two parts. Part 1 is all about understanding The Indian mindset and part 2 covers various business sectors like Real estate, Retail, BPO, Education, etc.

I hope this book will give you the insight into the Indian psychology, their business environment and help you to avoid costly mistakes while doing business in India.

With Best Regards

Subodh Gupta

Part 1

Understanding the Indian Mind

What motivates Indian people most?

What do you think is the **best** motivator for most people in a country like India, a country which is considered a land of spirituality?

Take a one minute break here, think and test your knowledge about Indian people's minds...

.

.

.

Good, so now you have done your homework and decided what best motivates the Indian mind, be prepared for the answer.

Well, the answer is very simple: **M**oney

You must be *smiling* and wondering what is so special about it. Around the globe *money* is one thing which motivates everybody, but you already knew that.

However the difference lies in how ***p**assionately* people in India seek money and what *they can do to obtain it.*

People talk about money and business in their offices and business meetings around the globe and I understand that this is perfectly natural. However, the passion of Indian people for money is really remarkable.

Let us see how:

- *They **love** it and talk about it **everywhere,***

 *-P**ray for money** every morning,*

*-Try to involve **G**od **into business partnership,***

*-Their **BPO gets** involved into **smuggling drugs,***

*-**Doctors** can **steal kidneys,***

*-Actors and directors do **human trafficking** and*

*-Even **their spiritual gurus** …only **for money.***

Love it...

Indian people love money so much that they talk about it everywhere, all the time. They talk about it in marriages, parties, general meetings, during dowries (a *social unspoken evil custom in India where the bride's parents give money to the groom and his parents before marriage so that their daughter can be happy and the groom or his parents may not harass her*), during sport events, even during casual meetings. For example, *if you come across an Indian gentleman even for the first time, please don't be surprised if within minutes he asks you how much you are earning* and how he can benefit.

The social custom in India <u>is such</u> that everything is based on how rich you are. One's only measure of success is how financially well off you are and accordingly you <u>are respected</u> in society.

In marriages, parties and social gatherings people will be happy to talk to you and welcome you if you are rich enough according to their own standard and vice versa. It appears as if there is no other parameter of success in this spiritual country. People will praise you if you are financially well off, and these same people would forget who you are should your financial status change.

Pray for it every morning...

If you go to any office in India or any showroom or shop and look around carefully you would notice a small place where *every Indian businessman goes in the morning to pray to the mother Laxmi (Goddess of Money) with the belief that by praying to goddess Laxmi he would earn more* and his sales would improve …

If this is not enough to amaze you, then read on further. There is a famous temple in India where Indian people offer a **business** *partnership to God*.

I am not joking! People go to this famous temple and offer a deal to God that, "if my business deal …or if I earn …then I would offer this much % of money as a donation".

And guess what, *this particular temple is the richest temple in India and probably in the world.*

You might be surprised to learn that "*Donations given by devotees equal nearly $2 million every month. Auctions of human hair fetched revenue of $25 million; temple admission ticket sales fetched revenue of $25 million in 2007*"[1]. Not only that, but TTD (an independent trust which manages the Tirumala Venkateswara Temple) *approved an unprecedented* **$500 million budget** *for the fiscal year 2008*[1]. Huge crowds and queue management are done with Tata Consultancy Services software and hardware infrastructure along with other companies.

BPO into smuggling drugs...

Narcotics Control Bureau (NCB) raided an Indian BPO in Noida on Monday and arrested two persons for smuggling drugs to the US...The BPO, situated in Sector 63 in Noida, is the **second call centre found engaged in drug smuggling**[2].

Doctors stealing Kidneys in India...

Some people in India can go to any lengths to make large amounts of money in a short time. *"Doctors steal 500 kidneys in Incredible India "*[3], *"After Dr Death and Dr Kidney, Dr Greed"*[4].

Actors and directors into human trafficking...

If you think only the common man is running the race for big money within a short time, then think again; even Indian film personalities are not far behind.

In March 2008, a racket involving south Indian film actors and directors was busted for human trafficking and American administration has slapped a lifetime ban on nearly 200 personalities from the film industry from travelling to the US. *US visa racket involving film industry unearthed* [5].

So what is the outcome in a situation where people want money so passionately?

"4 Indians in Forbes' top 10 billionaires list"[6]

I don't feel surprised when I read the above news headlines in the media as these are so obvious to me.

Even spiritual gurus…

Even spiritual gurus in India are running the race to make big money and achieve fame. Take any guru wearing orange clothes and you would find that he is running a million dollar organization.

But they do it differently. They open a non profit organization and rather than taking money from the public by selling tickets or membership fees, they have a concept of "suggested" donation so they are exempt from paying taxes however they charge the same amount of money for the membership fee in the name of helping people and also get government land at subsidised prices or even free & so on.

Exceptions…

However, there are always exceptions. A few organizations based in India like Vipassana meditation (www.dhamma.org) founded by respected teacher Shri S.N. Goenka, are doing commendable work around the globe without any money or fame, just for the sake of happiness and peace for humanity. Thousands of people have joined this organization in India as well as around the globe helping themselves and others.

Point to remember: Indians are *highly passionate* about making big money in the shortest time possible. It *is their biggest motivator* because their social status will go up, they can boast about how rich they are with friends, relatives or whoever they meet.

Negotiations in India

Think for a moment how many times you negotiate with somebody in one day or within a month?

I hardly remember needing to negotiate at anytime during the last 3 years of my stay in London, except while dealing with estate agents to rent a house. Otherwise I find life simple.

Now guess how many times people would have negotiated in a time span of 3 years in India?

Well, I would say at least 1000 times and this is no exaggeration, because in India people negotiate for everything. The moment people wake up in the morning they go to the local food market and they start their day negotiating *with vegetable and fruit vendors.*

They negotiate with any service provider, whether it is a plumber, a carpenter or a cleaner, etc.

They go shopping and they negotiate for everything, such as clothes, shoes, TV, fridge, computer, etc.

They negotiate while dealing with ad agency suppliers, their chartered accounts, lawyers, etc.

Now think for a moment and tell me who you think would be the expert in negotiation: an Indian or a person who hardly does any negotiation?

There is an underlying feeling in the mind of Indian consumers that if you do not negotiate while purchasing, that means you have overpaid, so they negotiate everything. Shopkeepers and

18

service providers also understand this and therefore put a higher price on all their products.

If you are a foreigner in India, there is a very high possibility that a shopkeeper or a taxi driver would have already doubled the price the moment they saw you. If you purchase from a big showroom or book your taxi from a 4 or 5 star hotel the prices are fixed however; prices at these places are already well above the general market price.

Real life Situation during Negotiation

Tom, an educationist, was going back to the UK from India and was busy packing and selling all his belonging before leaving. He kept his car until the last moment as he needed it for mobility.

The day before his departure he went to the car market at Karol Bagh in New Delhi where he could sell his car instantly. This is a car market where you can sell your vehicle immediately, but of course the prices would be at least about 20 to 30 percent less as you come under the category of a desperate seller.

Tom had an idea what price he could sell his car for and *reduced the price by about 30 percent,* as he was in no mood to bargain. He wanted to sell quickly so that he could carry on with his other work.

He approached the car dealer who dealt with on the spot purchases and told him that he was leaving the next day and needed to sell his car immediately.

The car dealer took the car for a test drive and got it checked over with his experts. He gave Tom a price which was at least a further 25 % less than the one which Tom was asking for.

Tom wanted to sell, but not at such a low price, so he refused saying he would prefer to try other places. As he was about to leave the dealer asked him to wait for a moment as he knew somebody who might be interested in buying his car.

Tom agreed and waited impatiently until the potential buyer arrived 15 minutes later. The Buyer looked at the car and offered a price 40 % less than what Tom was originally asking for.

Tom refused, and the car dealer called another person within the next 5 minutes and he also offered 40 % less.

Tom refused again *and thought it would be better if he gave the car as a gift to his Indian friend rather than selling it at very low price.* However, he was confused at why the car dealer valued his car at 25 % less than that of the *already reduced* price he quoted and why the other 2 buyers offered a further 40 % less.

Suddenly he realised something and he asked the buyers a few questions which they couldn't answer. Only to find out that they were not actual buyers, but his own employees working at his other showroom, who were brought in as fake buyers in order to reduce the price.

Points to remember:

(1) Tom didn't want to negotiate as he was in a hurry and quoted a price which he thought was low enough. He believed that the car would be sold instantly, but didn't understand the Indian psychology that *no matter what price he would ask for they would always negotiate.*

(2) In the *unorganised sectors of India, like car sales & purchase market and* **especially real estate** *sales & purchase, the practice of bringing in fake buyers* to reduce the price is very common and one needs to be fully aware of this while negotiating. *Also the people in sales & purchase of property are practical psychologists as they deal & negotiate with many customers every day. They have perfected the art of negotiation.* However, there are always exceptions as in my experience these dodgy practices in India would be less common or nonexistent if you dealt with people who are educationists and intellectuals.

(3) Indian businessmen do a lot of research about the person whom they are dealing with before making any final deals. Even in a casual conversation they try to get as much information as possible by asking numerous questions.

Where do Indian people spend most of their life savings?

There are six main areas where Indians (middle income group) spend most of their income & life savings in the following order:

(1) **Education for their children**
(2) **Daughters' marriages**
(3) **House**

(4) **Yellow gold**
(5) **(Status symbol) car**

Indians are well aware that they would spend the majority of their income in the first five areas, so they save well. The sixth area where Indians spend their money is: health.

(6)**Health**

This is the one area where Indian people spend money *unhappily* both for prevention of disease and its cure. They will be spending for years to come *unless they wake up and take action now.*

Let's understand each of them separately.

(1) Education for their children

Parents in India can spend any amount of money on their children's education. They can cut down their own expenses, but feel happy that their child can study in good (private) schools.

Indian people, especially the middle classes, don't mind if they are not able to go on holidays even once in every three to four

22

years, but their child's education should not suffer. Whether it involves a hefty donation for admission to reputable private schools, high fees, extra coaching costs or maybe taking a loan for their children's studies, they won't mind sacrificing their own dreams for their children's education. That's why you can see the following news in the media *"India now number 2 provider of overseas students to the UK"* and the total number of Indian domiciled students was over 19,000 in 2005/06.[7]

"India is already number one in the world in sending students to the United States for higher education".[8]

Reasons why Indians spend so much on their children:

The major reason is of course attachment and love for their children. Parents in India are ready to sacrifice their life in exchange for the pleasure they will have when their children are well educated and enjoy a good social status.

Also, for most of the middle class Indians, this is the only way to be able to come out of a life of mediocrity especially now as the foreign companies are coming to India, I can clearly see that salaries in India have gone up at least 200 to 400 % in the last four to five years, therefore justification for the education expenses have become all the more relevant.

Point to remember: Indian people don't hesitate to spend a major part of their income on their child's education if they can. They are even willing to take out loans, if that can give their child a good education. You will see the continuous rise in number of Indian students who are coming to study in the UK, US and Australia.

(2)Marriage

Preparation for marriages in India takes place at least six months in advance. This is the time when all the families and friends are invited and gather together. Small marriage parties can have a gathering of about 200 to 300 people, and big marriage parties in India can have a gathering of thousands.

Middle class parents in India spend a major part of their life savings on their daughter's marriage. Higher income group Indian people spend money for what they call 'social prestige'.

The more money they spend, the more people will talk about them and the prouder the parents will feel. Sometimes the bride's parents feel obligated to spend more because of the unspoken societal pressure. Ultimately it is parents of the bride-to-be who bear the maximum financial burden and if they are not rich enough, they live with the debt for many years to come after the marriage of their daughter.

There is also an *evil custom* known as a *dowry* which is still a big burden in Indian society. The concept started hundreds of years ago and the point was to give a newly married couple some financial support. This was provided by both the groom and bride's parents, was within their financial capacity and was given with their happiness. However this concept was manipulated by greed and developed within the Indian society over the years. *In India, mostly after marriage, the woman goes to live with the husband and his parents in a joint family.* The parents of the groom started asking for money from the parents of the bride, and somehow society accepted this as the norm because of greed.

Over the years, the demands kept on rising from the groom's parents and if the bride and her parents couldn't fulfil the demands, the bride would be physically and mentally abused and sometimes even burnt alive.

At one stage (around 1975-85) bride burning events due to dowry became so high that the Indian government had to take some action and made a strict law against a dowry, making it a serious offence. After that, the case of burning alive and abusing the bride has decreased, but is still not completely eliminated.

In fact, even now you can notice the following news headlines in the Indian media: *"Dowry death alleged"*[9] published on 23 rd Feb 2008, *"Woman beaten up for dowry"*[10] published on 29 Feb 2008, *"Man arrested for dowry harassment"* [11] published on 5 Mar 2008, *"Dowry death: Husband, in-laws detained"*[12] published on 24 Mar 2008, *"Rajkot woman stages semi-nude protest against dowry demand"*[13] published on 5 Jul 2007, etc.

The point to note here is that even after the enforcement of strict laws, only the cases of wife beating have come down. The demand for a dowry has not. In fact, it has increased over the years and is now demanded in a more subtle way.

Now every parent wants their daughter to be happy, so the parents of a bride do their best to raise as much money as possible. This puts lots of financial pressure on the parents and *in most cases the middle class and even upper middle class Indian families end up taking out loans which they are paying off for years after the marriage has taken place.*

The result is Indian people do not want baby girls. So what do they do? They go for illegal abortions and sometimes even kill the newborn girl. There were also some cases where the newborn girls were abandoned by their parents; *Newborn girl found on expressway*[14].

Deep inside, there is a huge pressure on Indian women when they get pregnant to deliver a male child. If it is a baby girl, many Asian women are forced to have an abortion.

If you think it may be happening only in small villages in India read the following: as per news published in the Guardian UK, *"Desperate British Asians fly to India to abort baby girls"*[15]. It is happening in the UK as well, where numbers of Asian women go to India for an abortion of their female child. *"As many as 13 million female foetuses may have been aborted in India in the past two decades following prenatal gender checks"*[15]. This has resulted in lower female to male ratio in India. *"No girls, please, we're Indian: India now has the dubious distinction of being known as the country that likes to ensure that girls are never born."*[16]. According to the 2001 Indian census, *"there are 927 girls for every 1,000 boys in the 0-6 age range"*.[17] This explains a lot about *sex related crimes against Western women in India.* **Point to remember**: Indian people spend a big part of their life savings on their daughter's marriage.

(3)House

After spending regular income on a child's education and a major part of their life savings on daughter's marriage, the rest of the savings are invested by Indian families into buying their house.

Indian families will take as big a loan as possible to make their house look good. One of the reasons for this is to enhance their social prestige. You might often find Indian people talking proudly about their house in statements such as *"I have imported marble from Italy….."* or *"My house is in such and such …… area"* or *"it is built up on …….. so many sq meters"*, etc.

(4) Yellow Gold

Apart from a house investment, Indians have a huge attachment to yellow gold and this is where they love to invest in huge quantities.

(5)Cars

After investing in gold, having a car is the next status symbol which every Indian dreams of.

I can remember that around 1991 having a small car was a big dream and a status symbol even in metropolitan area in India. The newly recruited class 1 government officer used to get a salary of about Rs 5000 ($125) a month, and the salary in the private sector was even less. At that time the price of a small car was about Rs 2 lakh ($5000) and was out of reach for almost all working class Indians, *if they worked honestly* and was certainly only a dream.

However, now everything is changing in India and the salaries of young graduates are starting at minimum of $300 to $ 500 in BPO industry.

In the IT sector in India, newly graduated engineers get around $600 per month (*if from IIT engineering college in India then starting salary could be even $2000 to $ 4000 a month*) and with 2 to 3 years experience one can easily have a salary of about $1000 to $2000 per month, courtesy of multinational organizations in India.

The small car prices are still the same i.e. about $5000, so guess what is happening… yes you are thinking correctly, every Indian is running towards owning a car.

On top of that, now one of the India's largest business groups has unveiled the TATA NANO car model at $2500 only, so you can easily predict what the situation on Indian roads is going to be in few years time.

This is not all - *most Indians have a special habit of flaunting and boasting about what they have personally* or what belongs to their family *and even what they don't have,* (at least in north India I have seen it for years), so big car companies get the benefit.

For Indians who are becoming upwardly mobile, big car companies are introducing newer and newer car models to satisfy the appetite of the Indian masses and selling successfully. I don't even want to think what is going to happen to Indian city roads within a few years.

(6)Health

This is one area where I could see the medical industry in India flourishing for years without recession and where Indian people will be spending a major part of their savings.

There are five main reasons in my opinion why Indian people would be falling ill in numbers in the coming years unless they take action now.

(1) Indian people are *physically* lazy.

(2) They eat lots of *junk (Indian)* food.

(3) Lots of Indian *food is adulterated* and the water supply is also substandard.

(4) U*nhealthy western fast food* is infiltrating into Indian markets in a big way.

(5) Air and noise pollution

Indians are ph**ysically lazy**

People in India are **very active mentally,** but are *physically lazy*. They don't want to make any physical effort. A clear example is the Olympic games results; *Indian constitutes almost world 1/6th population and not a single Olympic gold medal has been won since the last 15-20 years or maybe more.*

There is an interesting concept in India that if you have a big belly it means you are wealthy. You could go to any Indian city and notice Indian men with big bellies moving around very happily and this would be the cause of many diseases in the coming years. *I have seen in the past years, 2000 to 2005, that a number of entrepreneurs have opened new GYMs in various locations in Delhi city and wondered why they are losing money.*

Most of these gym owners were bodybuilders with a passion for fitness and thought of converting it into business as well. The majority of gym owners ended up closing down their gyms. The reason for the failure of gyms in Delhi was the people's habit of not partaking in physical exercise.

So what happens when you don't do physical exercise to keep your body fit? Your health care expenses will certainly increase after the age of 30 to 35.

Indian junk food

There is lots of junk food in India which is tasty, no doubt, but quite dangerous for the health.

The sweet food like jalebi , burfi, gulab jamun and salty samosas, etc. are eaten in bulk in lower income group Indian households during festivals and almost daily in middle and higher income group. Hence lots of diseases and extra weight around belly.

Adulterated Indian food:

This is another shameful act committed by Indians to the Indians. In order to earn quick money, they don't even hesitate to destroy the health of others. There have been numerous incidents I have read in the past where vendors were adulterating almost every food in India to gain more profit.

Let's have a look

*"Chemical tea: Train passengers sip slow poison…*Hundreds of people drink tea at the Aurangabad railway station every day, but perhaps they don't know that what they are sipping is really a concoction of chemicals".[18]

Recently there were raids all over Mumbai searching for adulterated milk. When one Mumbai homemaker identified that the milk supplied to her house was adulterated *"Mumbai homemaker busts milk adulteration racket."*[19]

In a shocking revelation, the Food and Drug administration (FDA) Mumbai has said that "nearly 25 % of the milk produced in the state is adulterated."[20]

Food adulteration is not a recent incident in India, it has been happening for years. For example, according to a news article published in The Times of India Hyderabad in 2002:*"There might be iron filings in the sugar you use, including what is distributed through fair price shops all over the state. Food grains could also be infested by worms at the Food Corporation of India (FCI) godowns and fair price shops".*[21]

In 2003 in Patna (Bihar): *Hotel owner fined in food adulteration case*[22].

There are hundreds of news headlines which highlight the fact that food adulteration is going on in India in a rampant way. The reason for a high rate of food adulteration is, as I have previously explained, that people are highly passionate about earning lots of money in the shortest possible time and are ready to do whatever is required. Apart from Indian people's passion for money, *The Prevention of Food Adulteration Act (PFA) is not exactly consumer-friendly in India. Vegetables with artificial colours are a common sight. Even fruits are not spared. Watermelons are injected with colour to redden the pulp[23].*

And don't forget that it is not only the food, but the water supply which is also substandard. This is not just my opinion; it was admitted by the Union Government itself. *Delhi water substandard: Govt* [24]

Now think what will happen to Indian people's health when the milk they drink is mixed with chemicals, sweets are adulterated, vegetables are mixed with artificial colours, fruits are injected with colour and water is also substandard, etc?

Unhealthy Western fast foods

As the income level of a young Indian generation is increasing fast their spending habits are also changing.

Of course, they are getting addicted to western fast food joints in metro cities.

This results in eating fast food like pizzas and burgers which contains empty calories with lots of saturated fat (*For example A Tomato Mozzarella & Provolone Pizza (V) of 330 g can have* **730 K calorie and** *about* **25 g fat,**11.6 g *saturated*) which will result in weight gain and ultimately in various diseases.

Air & noise pollution:

In my opinion, the city of Delhi is (surely) moving towards air and noise pollution disaster. Delhi is a city where about 14 million people live with a population density of 9340 per sq km (9340 people live in 1 sq km of area), and has about 4 million vehicles on the roads with *nearly 1,000 new private vehicles being added to Delhi's roads every day[25]*. These numbers are going to jump up further when the TATA group world's cheapest car at $2500 is going to hit the Indian market.

Now imagine 1000 new vehicles are added every day to the roads of Delhi. Guess what would happen in one year's time: there would be 3,65,000 new vehicles and nearly 2 million extra vehicles on the road within the next 5 years.

Roads of Delhi city are already choked with the traffic. I remember that driving a distance of about 20 km in Delhi could easily take about 1 hour in 2005 and the situation is only going from bad to worse with so much traffic. The time to travel from one place to another in major cities is increasing like anything. *Traffic speed in Mumbai dropped from an average of 38 kmph in 1962 to 15-20 kmph in 1993; in Delhi from 20-27 kmph in 1997 to 15 kmph in 2002; and in Kolkata's heart to 7 kmph in 2002[26].*

Do you think that air quality would deteriorate? Of course it would. In fact it has already become worse. *Environmentalists say an estimated 2,000 metric tonnes of air pollutants are released into the atmosphere every day in New Delhi, one of Asia's most polluted cities.[27]*

The CSE says the high pollution levels lead to greater risks of respiratory illnesses such as **asthma** *and* **bronchitis** *and also* **heart disease.**[25]

Although government CNG (Compressed Natural Gas) programme has made a difference to air quality, the rising number of vehicles on the roads has undone that effort.

Delhi, India's capital is not the only case. According to another report published on BBC News, *Air pollution suffocates Calcutta; Some* **70% of people in the city of Calcutta suffer from respiratory disorders caused by air pollution**, *a recent study by a prominent cancer institute in India has concluded.*[28]

Now think about Mumbai, the financial capital of India. Recently **Forbes magazine named Mumbai as city of junk**[29].

Another news headline in the Financial Times read, **"Indian cities ranked last for air quality"**[30].

Noise pollution is another thing which is going to increase like anything in India.

As the number of cars and other vehicles increases, so does the noise pollution. If you are going from the UK to India you would get a big shock seeing the driving and traffic on city roads. While on the roads in the UK people use the horn only when it is necessary and you rarely hear that noise, in India it is different. The first thing people use is a horn and they are quite impatient, therefore, noise pollution is also increasing day by day.

Now imagine a country where the citizens are highly stressed *because of their children's education and daughters marriage,* where air pollution is so high that its metro cities are ranked last in air quality, 70 % people of one of the main metro cities suffer from respiratory disorder, 1000 new vehicles are being added to roads every day on another city, people are fond of eating high calorie junk food , its own food is adulterated by greedy citizens with chemicals and on top of that people do not exercise- *what will happen to people's health?*

Let's have a look at what the news says; ***Indians in bigger risk of diabetes***[31],

India is world's TB capital; *Over six lakh (6,00,000) Indians, unaware that they suffer from tuberculosis, are spreading the disease among healthy individuals*[32],

India among world's top hot spots of deadly emerging diseases[33], ***India's rapid economic growth could be slowed*** *by a sharp rise in the prevalence of* ***heart disease, stroke and diabetes***[34].

Yes, you are thinking correctly. Sad, but it is true. The diseases mentioned would spread all over India going by my analysis if these conditions continue to persist. People would fall ill in numbers and of course the hospital or medical industry would grow at an unprecedented rate in India.

Point to remember: Indian people would be spending a major part of their earning in curing various diseases and the hospital or medical industry would be thriving for years to come without any recession.

The culture of saving money

Indians have a great saving habit and somehow it is part of the culture and it is growing. *"India's saving rate is relatively high, compared with that of other countries. It has shown an uneven upward trend over the past four decades"*[35].

"Indians saved a total of Rs 7,58,751 crore in FY07."[36] (approximately 189.68 Billions US dollars; considering Rs 4000 crore = 1 billion US Dollar approx).

I can see three main reasons for the saving habits among Indian people.

The first reason is necessity; if you have read the earlier topics on *education* and *marriages* you can easily deduct the inference from reading that Indians save a lot because they end up spending a large amount of their money on their daughter's marriages, dowry and children's education, which is more or less essential in their minds.

The second reason is that Indians play it safe. They plan a lot for their old age and Indian businessmen prefer to have a cushion of savings just in case something goes wrong in business.

The third reason; They feel happy and content that they have so much money saved in their bank locker and they are rich, therefore society gives them more respect.

The point to note here is that people feel happy and proud to have great savings in their bank accounts or their bank lockers and they don't mind even though they may not have the necessary basics for comfort in their houses.

You might argue then, how come every day more than 1000 new cars are coming on the roads of Delhi?

Well that's right, but having a car is something they can show off to their neighbours and feel happy thinking that their image is improving otherwise they prefer to save and spend money only where it is necessary and useful.

Where do Indians save money?

In general Indian people prefer to invest the money in yellow gold and buying more and more properties. *"Indians prefer their savings in the form of physical assets instead of financial instruments and this trend is likely to continue despite the India growth story"*[37].

Most of the Indians have passion for yellow gold and they think whatever money they invest in gold is safe. So when they find surplus money they prefer to purchase gold.

Unlike the western countries, the craving for an average Indian to have yellow gold is so astonishing that he will go for it even if it meant not having the essential comfort of living and this is the reason that India is one of the biggest consumer of yellow gold all over the world and prices of gold in India are high.

Some of the readers may not agree with my statement when I say Indians prefer saving mainly in physical assets thinking that as per the figures available to you, there is not much difference in savings of Physical Assets vs financial assets in India. Yes figures may not show much difference but the fact is *Indian real estate market is highly opaque and investment in property shown on paper is highly undervalued 100 % to 200 %, and could be much more in some cases (as lots of "black money" is involved) for the tax purpose i.e. figures may not show the actual scenario in India sometimes.*

People saving interest in financial assets is also increasing as the number of banks and life insurance branches are opening in remote areas, i.e. save in bank deposits, life

38

Insurance policies, etc *but Indian people **in general** play safe even when it is about saving* and for them safety is more in physical assets.

Point to remember: Indians prefer to invest in yellow gold and properties.

Note: If you are interested in understanding more about Indians mind, **their culture** and practical guidelines in **bridging the communication gap**, you may refer to my book " ***Understanding Indian Culture and Bridging the communication gap;** available on Amazon and Barnes and Nobles, ISBN: 978-0-9556882-5-6* ".

Part 2

Doing Business in India

&

Understanding Pitfalls

Myth about 300 million middle class Indians Purchasing power

Sometimes I am really surprised when I hear or read the news that there is some strong 300 million middle class consumer base in India who has almost same purchasing power as middle classes income group people in USA or in Europe.

Well to put it straight, I completely disagree and would like to say *that there is no such 300 million middle class consumer base in India who has same purchasing power as middle income group European or American at least till now year 2008.*

Also the spending power of middle and high income group Indians is highly overestimated by experts from eminent consulting organizations.

The reason for this is that people who are making these reports sit in their offices without ever actually going out to the Indian marketplace and have never tried to look into the Indian consumer mind.

Let's understand the myth of high purchasing power;

In India till now the total number of people who pay income tax is about only 31.5 million that is only about 3 % of the total Indian population. *India has 31.5 million taxpayers; In a country of over a billion people, only 31.5 million people pay taxes, and this is after the number of taxpayers has grown by nearly 11 percent between March 2002 and March 2006*[38]. Now in India people start paying tax only when their income goes above Rs 1,00,000 or £1250 per year (*£1 = 80 Rupee approx)* (*this is the person income tax exemption limit till last year 2007 in India for men*).

So as per Indian Govt Tax official estimate only about 3 % of Indians earn more than £1250 per year or about £100 per month. Now£100 per month is nowhere close to European or American middle class earning standard, than assumption that *India have 30 % or 300 million middle class populations who have same purchasing power as people in USA or Europe??? At least I can't understand.*

I knew that some readers might be thinking that as per hearsay not everyone pays taxes in India and some people declare less income than they actually have. Ok let's say you are right and I gave you the benefit of doubt to the extent of even 100%, still the number of people in tax bracket do not exceed more than 6 % of total population and still nowhere around 30 % of Indian total population as calculated by some experts.

Also that 6 % population is only earning above £100 per month and the point is even within that 6% or 60 million Indians not everybody have the *same purchasing power as people in the middle income group in the West.*

So all the big MNC companies who enter into Indian retail market looking at the sheer numbers of population face huge disappointment as the number of Indians who have the same purchasing power as European or American may be hardly 1 % or 1.2% i.e. about 10 to 12 million only.

Another issue for the retail sector is that this 10 - 12 million consumer of high income group is not located in the small pocket of India but all over India which is as large as Europe so distribution is another issue because country infrastructure is almost bleeding.

Another point which a luxury consumer goods company like Mercedes or Audi may not like is that the people who have the money but don't declare it would not be able to purchase their expensive luxury cars as for purchasing any luxury car you need to show money in white i.e. on papers, which many in India don't, so they cannot purchase even though have the money.

Overestimated Indian market potential...

Experts who make big news about high purchasing power of Indian high income group *only tell about growth rate in India* which seems impressive but in actual terms that comes out to be almost nothing.

Let's look at the sales of the German luxury car group BMW in the first quarter of 2008.

According to a news article, "*The biggest increase for BMW was in India, where there was a leap of 800 per cent... Sales fell however by 9.2 percent in the United States,*"[39] now this looks impressive isn't, 800% jump in India and gives a rosy picture about Indian growing market.

Now let's look at the total number of cars sold in India, well it is only 862 BMW cars sold in whole of India in first quarter of 2008? Do you think it is a very big market???

I can imagine you are thinking that it is growing market and rate of jump 800% is significant but if you look at the base upon which 800% is calculated, that was only about 90 cars last year which is insignificant and in number terms the actual sales of cars have only increased by about 760 cars only.

Understanding the Indian market, I could easily say that for the next years the % growth figure would never look like 800% rather it would come down sharply.

Let's look at the number of BMW car sold in the US in an economy which seems to be going down in 2008. *The total of 68,500 BMW cars were sold in the three month period in the US.*[39]

Is there any comparison between the Indian and the US market???

Let's have a look at Aviation sector in India which is another promising sector and making big news in India and Internationally about its big potential.

I remember during 1990 -1993 the air ticket for Delhi to Bangalore was about Rs 10000 to Rs 12000 (about $300) and the salary of newly recruited class 1, Indian government official was around Rs 5000 ($125) a month and it certainly was a big dream even for a senior official to travel by air in India. It was mostly the business magnates in India that used to travel by air at that time.

However, now the situation is completely changed. The salary of Indian professionals has gone sky high. The starting salary for a entry level engineer has easily gone up to minimum $600 dollars a month and if from a reputed college like IIT, the starting salary has gone up to $2000 to $3000 a month.

The ticket price for air travel has drastically come down to $100 to $150 dollars after about 15 years and if you book in advance the price for air ticket in India were even about $ 40 to $ 50 for the same Delhi and Bangalore route till a few weeks before oil crises.

 As millions of jobs have been imported into India from all over the world, certainly the income level of people in India has improved a lot.

Since air travel for most of the Indians was a dream, so don't you think that all the domestic air craft must be full with Indians because of their big populations, and Indian airlines must be earning huge profits, isn't it?

Well the fact is that no doubt the number of air passengers in India has considerably increased and numbers do look very impressive but **coming back to spending powers of middle class Indians,** if we look at recent news about profits of airlines in India, the situation is *"Airlines in India have suffered a staggering loss of Rs 4,000 crore (Rs 40 billion) in 2007-08, and it could double in the current fiscal depending on which way fuel prices are headed, Civil Aviation Secretary Ashok Chawla said"*[40].

I knew that optimists in the aviation industry who created the hype would say that growth will take care of the problems, as India has the fastest-growing number of passengers in the world but then why domestic airline industry in India is cutting the flights and slashing their capacity. *" the worst slowdown in the Indian aviation industry since 2004, airlines have decided to withdraw 165 flights in the last four weeks, slashing their total capacity by around 10 per cent"?*[41]

The point I want to make here is that now, *at a time when many Indian airlines had predicted that they would be profitable, the industry is still losing money and number of operators are struggling to meet day-to-day expenses* and have decided to cut non profitable sectors. The entire airline industry in Indian domestic sector is operating with fares below their costs as **Indians middle class are extremely price conscious** and still do not spend as expected.

Despite the fact that Indians salary has increased many folds and the prices of air tickets in India have come down by 50% to 70 %, the industry is still suffering.

Point to remember: There is no such strong 300 million middle class consumer base in India who has almost same purchasing power as middle classes income people in USA or in Europe.

Only about 3% Indians, i.e. 31.5 million Indians pay taxes.

India is almost as big as the whole of Europe and the distribution or supply chain system is unreliable.

There is no comparison in markets between the US and India, *despite the fact Indian population is more than 3 times US population and US economy is showing sign of going down.*

The Indian middle and high income group's spending habit is highly overestimated by experts from eminent consulting organizations.

On the parameter of **ease of doing business**, India rank at 120th place out of 178 world economy, well below Vietnam 91, Bangladesh 107, Nigeria 108, Nepal 111 and China 83.

Singapore ranked at no 1 rank, US at rank 3 and the UK at rank 6.

(The first place being the best, a high ranking on the ease of doing business index means the regulatory environment is conducive to the operation of business).
Source: Doing Business 2008 (by World Bank Group)

48

Retail Sector

India is considered as one of the most attractive retail market in the world now, which at the moment is dominated by unorganized domestic players.

Organised retail, which accounts for $12.4 billion only in year 2006 which is 4.6 % of the $ 270 billion Indian retail sector, is expected to grow at 37 % in 2007 and 42 % in 2008. [42]

Slowing growth and decreasing profits in the foreign domestic market is pushing foreign retailers to Indian market, which promises immense market potential as number looks impressive.

However, *I believe without proper understanding the Indian retail gold mine, rushing to the Indian market can be the prime reason for failure*.

Indian retail market is characterised by vast differences in purchase power and footfalls. Whatever level the income of people in India rises, I believe majority of *Indian consumers still want value for their money and also quite price conscious.*

Let's see the various pitfalls in Indian retail sector.

There are many area which acts as potential hurdles in expanding organized retail market in India. For example: Real estate hurdles, inadequate Infrastructure, under developed supply chain capabilities, insufficient government incentives & policy-related hurdles.

Among all the above major hurdles, I understand real estate has become the biggest issue now if we look at the recent rental prices in major cities in India.

Rent for offices in cities like Mumbai has shot up to $150 per sq ft per year which is too high if compare to rent in cities like even Paris and New York etc. *"Mumbai : World's 4th most expensive office mart"*.[43]

The fact is that nowadays retailers in India are spending about 25-50% of their revenues only for rentals, just to operate in metropolitan cities.

Let's see with the help of practical examples how difficult it is to do retail business in India because of high rentals at the moment.

Project coffee shop for any international brand:

Location: South Extension part II or Greater Kailash II in New Delhi where people with high income group live.

Considering we need about 800 sq feet to 1000 sq feet area for a coffee shop. The prevailing rental rate on one of the Indian property portal magicbricks.com for these locations at the moment (year 2008)varies from Rs 2,00,000/- to Rs 4,00,000/- per month for a 1000 sq feet area.

Let's take an average rate of Rs 3,00,000 per month for 1000 sq feet of area. Rs 3,00,000 per month means about $7500 per month (considering 1 $ = Rs 40) or about £3750 pound per month (considering 1£ = Rs 80).

Considering rental cost as 30 % of total revenue, which gives us target turnover to be achieved from a single coffee shop per month to be Rs 10,00,000 ($25000) per month.

Considering market open for 6 days a week, say 25 days in a month, for earning Rs 10, 00,000 per month, say each day sales should be Rs 40000.

Now considering coffee shop opens for 10 hours a day that means, it needs to earn Rs 4,000 per hour.

Let's say on an average a customer spends Rs 50 on coffee cup and other sweets. This means every one hour the shop needs to sell 80 cups.

So 80 cups per 60 minutes means *within* every 45 seconds, *a order has to be taken, coffee has to be made, change has to be returned and coffee has to be served*, and if this process works ideally and goes on continuous for every minute, for the next 10 hours, every day, every week then you can run a coffee shop like star bucks but still with 30 % revenue as rental cost which as per my own business experience in India is highly improbable if you understand the Indian people mind.

Reason why this coffee shop model can fail:

(a)Indian people are not as habitual for drinking coffee before office hours as people in a city such as London. Also normally in all offices there are always free coffee machines in India.

(b)Even in a city like London where people habitually drink coffee, the coffee shops are not full during all the business hours.

Peak rate is during the early morning before office hours and then keeps on changing during the day.

If we take average occupancy of 50 % for the whole day which still means every one and a half minutes one customer is served on counter (which is still improbable in my own estimate) the turnover comes down to Rs 5,00,000 from Rs 10,00,000 per month i.e. which means now rental value will come out to be almost 60 % of revenue.

India is a land of surprises and there are many other factors which are always there which can affect the sales, ranging from various holidays, strikes, electricity issues, high attrition rate, etc.

In some cases the businesses are not able to recover even the rental costs *however the shops which sell the high value products and where the product is in big demand, profits can still be earned.*

This high rent in major cities would either leads to slowing down of expansion plan of major retailers or change of strategy.

Rentals are proving too high not only for small or medium size business in India but even for MNC like Adidas.

According to Adidas India, Managing director, Andreas Gellner, *"Rise in real estate prices have been affecting our growth plans in India"*[44]. Talking about real estate prices, he said that *"the prevailing rentals were not realistic...rentals at the moment were more than 20 per cent per square feet and in some cases it was around 40 per cent per square feet"* of the turnover.[44]

Now the interesting point here is that when most of the foreign retailers are planning to come to India to open shop and take share of Indian retail market, Indian restaurants owners think that Indian market is not profitable and are looking outside India for example, Dubai, US and the UK to do business as they are finding rental pricing in India unaffordable and less attractive.

Speaking on the investment returns ratio in India, Anjan Chatterjee a veteran restaurateur said that *"Yes, the prices that we have to pay in Mumbai and Delhi are exorbitant and we would rather invest in New York and Leicester. Not only do we have to invest less in real estate there, but the returns are much higher than what we get in India,"*[45]…

"The rate of return is also higher in the UK than in Mumbai and New Delhi," says Anuj Puri, head of Jones Lang Lasalle *Meghraj.*[45]

According to Dhruv Lamba, executive director, Kwality Group in India *"We are investing in London and the Middle East as it makes more sense, not only in terms of the prices but the returns as well,"*[45]

Other problems that are considerable hurdles in Indian retail markets are inadequate infrastructure, supply chain, a lack of a sustainable vendor base and trained manpower.

Apart from above hurdles in India, attitude of some of the Indian state government towards organized retail is also hostile because of vote politics as small trading community in unorganized sector forms a formidable vote bank which is against this organized retail sector.

This state government attitude is not only a headache for foreign MNC but even for a big Indian organization like Reliance. For example in mid 2007 number of state governments in India even bans the retails outlets of India's largest organization, Reliance because of opposition of peoples.

"After opposition in West Bengal, Tamil Nadu and Jharkhand to retail chains selling farm produce, it was the turn of Uttar Pradesh to slam its doors on Mukesh Ambani's Reliance Fresh stores and also RPG group's Spencer's".[46]

Shopping space in big shopping malls in India has been sold or rented out at big premium at places like Gurgoan, Delhi and Noida to various MNC and the price is largely based on footfalls and location.

However **consumer behaviour in India is very much different to that in the UK or the US.**

Many showroom owners who purchased big retail spaces ended up making losses and many more would in occur in the future.

The following are some of the advantages that shop owners in the Indian <u>un</u>organized retail sector have over MNC organized retail chains:

	Unorganized (Small shop Owners)	Unorganized Big showrooms	Organized MNC, Retail Chains
Rent	Normally shop owners in this category do not pay any rent for their shop as they make small extension for shop within their house. **NO Rent**	Indians usually purchase the shop as they think value of shop / property would further increase in coming years. (*Most of money paid in black i.e. . unaccounted money.*)	Usually take space on **exorbitant rent** in big shopping malls or big markets.
Salary to Staff	**No Salary** as shops are small and family members are taking care of shop.	Family members + few staff on salary. **But the salary of staff would be much less** as compared to that in the organized retail chain.	**At least 100 % to 400 % more salary** for the staff as compared to that in the unorganized sector.
Recruitment Cost	NIL	**Less** as compared to that in the organized retail chains	**Big recruitment cost.**
Attrition rate	NIL	**Very less** *as compared to that in the organized retail chains.* One reason is that staff would be	**HIGH Attrition Rate** As staff are more educated and keep an eye

		from low income group but hardworking and having less awareness of opportunity and growth.	on new job opportunities.
Training cost	**NIL**	Less as compared to organized retail chain as emphasise is more on training while doing i.e. mostly while on job.	Standard training and cost associated with it for training employees.
Relationship with customer	**More personal**	More personal as compared to organized MNC retail chain as owner or Entrepreneur take care of it personally.	Less personal as for employees it is not their whole life job. However could be more professional
Inventory	Usually ideals for small inventory size of up to 100 150 items	Can handle small to medium size inventory.	Can handle very large inventory.

If we look at the above table it become clear that it is difficult to compete with millions of small shops in unorganized retail sector in India as they don't have any rental cost, recruitment cost, salary cost, attrition cost, training cost etc. and they do maintain personal bonding with customer.

These small shops are located at very convenient location in small towns and cities and hence maintain regular sales. These shops mostly deal in very small value daily used products. The turnover of these shops is only good enough to give decent earning to small time retail entrepreneur.

It is the big shop owners in the cities who are mainly threatened with the arrival of MNC organized retail chains because these big shop owners do have some running cost but they don't have the big branding.

The MNC organized retail chains have some unique differentiating factors which gives them edge over big domestic retailers in India.

(a)Branding: Majority of people in high income group (1 % population i.e. 10millions people) loves to wear branded products and this is where organized chain have the edge.

(b)Consistent quality: Big brand also comes with consistent quality which in often missing in local Indian big retail showrooms.

(c) Foreign brands hold a big charm to the Indian consumer mind.

(d) Systems: I believe that systems used in running the organization are excellent in organized retail chains and can handle very big inventory.

(e) Deep pockets: Certainly organized chains have big pockets in comparison to local retail shops.

(f) Economy of scale: It is certainly in favour of big organized MNC retail organizations.

I realised over the years that for big profits margins, *either one should deal in high value products or work at mass scale* and I understand foreign multinational organized retail chain have both.

However, *following are some other points about behaviour pattern of Indian consumer which you (foreign investor) may need to consider before making investment in the Indian shopping malls or retail market.*

(a)People in India do not go to shopping malls just for buying the brands but rather most of them for window shopping, passing time and entertainment like movies, i.e. footfalls are not the correct criteria on which investment should be made in India.

(b)When it comes to house hold shopping, people in India prefers their local "trusted" vendor as compared to big shopping malls or at the most mix of both.

(c)**Price, quality** and **discounts** are the more important factor which influences purchasing decision except for 1 % top earning Indian population which may prefer brand or mixture of all above.

(d) Retail sector does not attract the best young talent as it does not involve foreign travel for most of employees.

Pitfalls in Retail Sector in India

The challenges that India retail sector faces are.

(1) **V**ery high rentals

(2) Inadequate Infrastructure,

(3) Inefficient supply chains,

(4) State government interference

(5) Lack of trained manpower

(6) Indian consumer behaviour

Solution: In my understanding for a foreign player franchise-driven operations will be more profitable in the Indian market in the near future for 2 reasons:

(1) The risk for foreign players is reduced.

(2) The local Indian players certainly understand the domestic market better than the foreign player and have lesser restrictions from government and would prove to be more competitive.

Dealing with PR agencies

When you are dealing with PR agencies in India, organizing the events for you, no matter how big it may be, remember to clarify which Indian national newspaper the journalist attending the event is from.

For example: 6 years ago a national level retail summit was organised in India for 3 full days in a 5 star hotel and India's leading PR agencies was managing the PR event.

Managing Director of the main sponsoring organization (MNC) to the summit gave his presentation about his product in a room which was full of journalists.

After the presentation, the MD celebrated with his global team present there the successful briefing to journalist anticipating good coverage. The sponsoring organization was very happy with the PR agency work as they had invited many journalists to the meeting.

Result: Surprisingly very little coverage in the major Indian national newspaper; reason there were only one journalist from the main newspaper, who did not stay for the whole presentation. She (journalist) came for couple of minutes collected the material about the presentation and left.

Little did the MD and his global team realise that the majority of the journalists sitting in the room were from small magazines and very small newspapers which did not focus on the target consumer and also hardly anyone of journalists were from major national newspapers.

However I think multinational organization have deep pockets and don't mind making such mistakes often in India, however, if you are doing business with a tight budget you need to clarify with your PR agency all the facts well in advance.

If you are an Entrepreneur and going to hire a medium size PR agency in India, following points will help you as reference.

Normally PR agency in India believes that generally an average client stays with them for an average of 8 to 10 months on retainer ship basis, so they try to offer as little as possible in lieu for a monthly fee so that you can stay longer.

 If you are a small entrepreneur and try to negotiate with them for coverage in the media, first they would try to lower down your expectation and their first dialogue would be that *"you are not Reliance or TATA group i.e. it would take about 2 to 3 months for building up relationship with media and then onwards results would start appearing"*.

Normally a medium size PR organization with about 6 to 10 employee used to charge about Rs 60000 to Rs 70000 per month (about £800) in year 2002-03 on retainer ship basis.

However as things has changed very fast in India in the last 3 to 4 years, I am sure the prizes must have gone up at least 100% percent.

India has been ranked 72 with CPI score 3.5 among 179 countries of the world on the worldwide Corruption Perceptions Index (CPI), prepared by independent international agency Transparency International.

UK occupies the 12th rank with CPI score 8.4 and US 20th spot with CPI score of 7.2[47]

CPI Score relates to perceptions of the degree of corruption as seen by business people and country analysts, and ranges between 10 (highly clean) and 0 (highly corrupt).

Source: Transparency International, Corruptions perception Index 2007

Real Estate

Over the last eight to ten years India has become one of the greatest economic success stories. The world biggest companies have been rushing towards India for investing in property market and to take a share of profits.

India's property sector has been booming along with other sectors like IT and according to one report prices in India for properties have increased 70% over the last two years.

This is one area which has made people millionaires in India in a very short time. The price of land and rent in *some* *specific* *locations* in metro cities like Delhi and Bombay has increased by 100% to 200 % in just 5 years within 2003 to 2008.

There are various reasons which contribute together for the high rise in property market in India.

(1)Outsourcing of millions of jobs to India

(2)Massive inflow of foreign Investment in India (because of predictions by world leading consulting companies)

(3)Opaque real estate sector and black money

(4)NRI and PIO Investments in India (fuelled by marketing seminars in foreign countries)

(5) Indian speculators and builders hype

Outsourcing of Jobs to India

One of the main reasons for rise in property value was massive inflow of jobs in India that took place initially because of vast salary difference in the West and India.

With the improvement in technology, companies all over the world realised that they can outsource most of the back office work to India to improve their profit margins, efficiency and cutting their cost.

India being one of the largest English speaking countries, with a technology savvy young generation with lesser salary became the hottest destination for companies all over the world.

Companies started shifting hundreds and thousands of jobs to India from all over the world and in this process the competition between the multinational companies itself went up for the right talent and so does the salary of young Indian professionals.

The salary of young Indian professional saw the astronomical growth perhaps the fastest in the world (*approx between 300 to 500 % in some particular professions and even more, within 2001 to 2008*).

With millions of job created in the Indian IT sector, the income level of the people increased.

This high income level along with Indians passion for acquiring more and more properties, leads to high prices of new homes and higher rents.

Massive inflow of foreign Investment in India

The other major reason for steep rise in land and rent in Indian market is because of massive inflow of foreign investment in India from around the world.

As the hundreds and thousands of jobs were created and salary of young Indians started rising up like never before, it is natural that their spending habits would also change, they would spend more and consumer goods market would get the boost.

So companies around the world now started looking towards India as the fastest new developing market for their products to sell especially when the market growth in Western market is almost stagnated.

So companies which are dealing in consumer goods markets started looking for opening their offices in India. Similarly companies which are dealing in real estate around the world found that India is going to be the hot destination in the coming time, so they started investing.

Now with hundreds of multinationals companies with deep pockets coming to India within a few years and looking for space in metro cities i.e. investment flow from all over the world towards India become massive and the rental value and price of land shoots up like anything.

Indians saw the steepest price rise in their property value ever in their life time and the major reason for this is that almost every multinational company has India on their list for some reason. It could be for investment purpose or as a market for their products or as their back office, etc.

However, I think one of the major reasons for the increase in property prices in India was the prediction and hype by the world leading consulting companies like *"Merrill Lynch whose consultant has predicted **a 700 per cent increase in the Indian property market by 2015"**[48]* and similar other prediction like *"**India will grow at about 8 per cent until 2020, according to a new report by Goldman Sachs"**[49]* which heavily boost the potential of Indian market in the mind of foreign investors.

This is one of the main reasons that so many foreign property funds and investors are pouring money into India.

"Already 25 US investment funds are raising US\$ 3.5 billion for investments in Indian realty. Those raising the funds include Wall Street companies such as the Blackstone Group (US\$ 1 billion) Goldman Sachs (US\$ 1 billion), Citigroup Property Investors (US\$ 125 million), Morgan Stanley (US\$ 70 million) and GE Commercial Finance Real Estate (US\$ 63 million).Others raising funds are JP Morgan, Warburg Pincus, Merrill Lynch, Lehman Brothers, Warren Buffett's Berkshire Hathaway, Colony Capital and Starwood Capital".[50]

As more and more companies are coming towards India hoping that they can make profits out of it, the property market has become the ***betting ground for foreign speculators*** and in this process the Indian property prices has shoot up.

Opaque real estate market and black money

India has a population of about 1000 million but hardly 3 % people pay the taxes.

The point I want to highlight here is that Indians have a huge amount of black money with them, which they cannot declare or invest where income is needed to be shown in white (on paper).

However, the real estate sector is still one area where a large amount of black money is invested because this sector is quite opaque.

For example if a flat is sold for Rs 5 millions, on papers it would be shown only for say 1 or 2 million rupees.

The rest of the money is transacted off the record and this practice is very obvious in the majority of property deals in India except where government itself is involved for sale and purchase.

Now with the recent steps by Indian central government in last couple of years to bring transparency in banking and other systems, it is very difficult for people in India to hide their black money in other areas except real estate.

Hence majority of the black money was shifted towards real estate market in India and this leads to rise in property market.

NRI (Non Resident Indians) and PIO (Person of Indian origin) Investment in India

If you enter into the mind of Indian people, you will find out that majority of NRI and PIO wants to have at least one property in their home land i.e. India, even though they live abroad *just in case.*

This psychology of the Indian mind was cashed by many marketing agencies in the UK, Europe and USA. These organizations organized hundreds of seminars luring investors to Indian property market.

Let's have a look at one of the *sales pitch* of property Investment firm offering new apartments in India suggesting investors (both Indian and foreigners) to Invest in India. *Reasons to invest in India – Some facts*[51]

 * 70% increase in Indian property prices over the last 2 years

 * 7 fold predicted increase in value of the property market from 2005-2015 (Merrill Lynch)

 * 300 million middle class people living in India by 2010 (higher than the US)

* 8% economic growth predicted until 2020 (Goldman Sachs)

* 19.8 million units housing shortage (Report from Gov of India) and 13.8% increase in wages in 2006 (highest in Asia-Pacific region).

These investment firms work on different revenue models. Some of the companies earn revenue by selling properties in India and getting commission.

Some would earn by providing other services in India like opening companies, furnishing houses and providing legal services.

Others by charging ticket price to attend seminars about doing business in India.

Main point is they would earn big profit _only_ when you would invest in India so they are highly motivated to motivate other people to invest in India and they try to put compelling statistics (partly true) to investors to lure them and they did succeed in their effort.

When NRI and PIO saw the compelling statistic and steep rise in price of properties in India, many of them rushed to India for investment purpose and which further fuelled the property market.

Speculators and builders hype

Everybody likes easy money, especially builders and speculators.

They created the artificial demand for their properties and earned huge premiums over the years and maintained the high price of properties.

But something unusual happened to the expectation of builders and speculators who already made millions of dollars. **The property bubble started bursting.**

Between mid of 2007 and start of year 2008 the prices stopped rising further and rather started falling moderately in all the major cities in India and in my understanding it will continue to fall further, about 10 to 20 % for at least another year.

What went wrong?

The combination of following factors helped in pulling the real estate price down.

Overpricing

Any price for a property can be maintained as long as the end users are available in the market but if the prices are too kept high, out of reach of majority of end users, prices are bound to fall, sooner or later.

Sales volumes of properties in main Indian metro cities fell sharply due to the high prices of apartments, which were kept beyond affordability levels for most people.

Some listed developers and agents were selling apartments at an average price of Rs 8million (approximately £100,000 pounds) @ Rs6,000/sq ft to Rs 7000/ sq ft which is way beyond the reach of majority of Indians.

Sensex has fallen by more than 30 % and realty stocks have fallen by more than 50% within few months from its peak in start of years 2008, including the stock of well respected companies like DLF and Unitech.

The fall of the reality stocks which is more than 50% shows that they were overpriced and artificial hype was maintained by the people who have interest in the respective companies share price, because if the growth is based on sound fundamentals, there cannot be more than 50% fall in few months.

Consistent overpricing of properties because of greed of property developers', agents and speculators is certainly one of the key factors in declining prices.

Liquidity

With high inflation and rising interest rates, demand for properties is further affecting in India.

People who had invested in the stock market have lost money because of falling stock market and do not have enough money to invest in the real estate. The liquidity crunch is started surfacing.

Non Resident Indians (NRI) and PIO

With the US property market witnessing a correction, the Non-resident Indians (NRIs) and PIO, who are the significant buyers for luxury properties in India, are expecting the same to happen in India and started holding back on their investment in Indian property market.

IT Industry

With uncertainty about US economy and slowdown in Europe, the space requirement of IT industry in India has been affected and I believe demand will remain weak in the near term.

Prices will further fall when government scheme of tax incentives to the companies in "technology parks" comes to an end.

Developers

Developers do not want to cut prices because once you do that, it signals the start of a downward spiral. They are holding on to the artificial prices to maintain the momentum but not all the developers are big enough to hold the prices and smaller developers started discounting the prices.

As big developers are hesitant at the moment to slash the prices, a downturn in sales seems unavoidable.

Speculators

Speculators sensing the market reality in India are already on run which become the another reason for very few takers of properties and hence the fall in prices.

Now with rising interest rate in India, speculators running away from the market, NRI holding back their investment back, IT Industry uncertain demand, developers overpricing and unwillingness to cut the pricing and liquidity crunch because of stock market falls, the situation has reached to this position that even in hot commercial market like Mumbai(Bombay), *"two of three commercial plots put up for auction by the Mumbai Metropolitan Region Development Authority (MMRDA) at the prime Bandra Kurla Complex has failed to find any takers*".[52]

This is a sign of the slowdown and correction in the commercial property market in India.

"Gulam Zia, national director for research and advisory services at Knight Frank...he added that price correction is inevitable as the current lease rents are not sustainable. "At present the prices are excessively jacked up,".[52]

There are many news reported within last 2 to3 months across the city confirming the downward trend in property price and sales in India.

"Property prices in Mumbai to fall by 15%"[53],..."*In my view, the price will go down by 10-15 per cent over the next six to nine months,*" Indiareit Fund Advisors' Managing Director and Chief Executive officer Ramesh Jogani said [53].

"*Real estate prices under pressure*",... *"The Reserve Bank of India's move to raise repo rates (the rate at which the RBI lends money to banks) is likely to trigger a further dip in realty prices over the next few months"*... *"We are heading for a major crisis. Prices have already crashed by 20 per cent. Nobody buys in a falling market expecting further correction. The repo rate will further aggravate the situation,"*[54] said Arvind Goyal, who heads Navi Mumbai-based real estate company Karnala Infra Projects.

"Speculative investors in real estate market are retreating, at least in the Delhi-NCR region"... *"A year ago, if we were selling over 100 flats in a month at launch stage, we now sell only 30-40 per month"*. Speculators, who would earlier frenetically

book flats at the pre-launch stage only, have now disappeared," said a senior executive of a real estate firm [55].

"DDA (Delhi Development Authority; Govt body) Struggling to Find Takers for Hotel Plots", ... "The authority has succeeded in selling only two of the seven plots put for auction" [56].

Now as buyers are retreating and waiting for further price cut, the supply of properties in many areas in India has exceeded the demand which is further adding to the fall in real estate prices in India.

"In Bangalore's Whitefield suburb, once a magnet for IT firms, supply outstripped absorption by 300,000 sq ft in 2007 and about 8% of the developed area remained vacant, data from real estate consultancy Cushman & Wakefield (C&W) show" [57].

"(OMR) technology cluster on the outskirts of Chennai is deep in the doldrums, with just nine deals in the whole of 2007. Of the four million sq ft that came into the market last year, only 1.7 million sq ft were absorbed even as rentals fell by 18% and the vacancy rate was up to 11%, again according to C&W data" [57].

All the above circumstances are leading the builders to a tough time in India. According to another news *"The real estate market has now moved from being under stress to a completely distressed condition."* ..."*A leading Mumbai-based developer who belongs to one of the country's leading construction families has backed out after offering Rs 700 crore (£ 87.5millions pound) to purchase the 18-acre Hindustan Composite land at LBS Marg in Ghatkopar*"[58].

The situation has become so difficult for builders that they even started defaulting the payment towards their land.

According to Mr Deepak Parekh, chairman HDFC bank, *"We have been hearing about this crunch. It's natural to happen. Builders have made land purchases, but the cash flow from the sale of flats has slowed down considerably because of high property prices. Despite the slowdown, they do not want to reduce prices. So, they default on payments towards land and also because they have borrowed money at exorbitant rates"*[58].

If you will ask about this situation to any reputed builder or developers in India, perhaps they would answer about this situation in a different way. For example their answer could be "The market is not falling, but stabilising and now we're seeing the real investors, people who will actually move in to these flats so it's a good thing".

Or you may get following reply, "There is really no big issue with the current fall in real estate prices as weak investors are getting panicky and pulling out and after they filter out price will rise again".

Whatever the answer developers give, reality is that, real estate prices were overly hyped in India and are moving towards downwards side or price correction.

Point to remember: So if you are planning to invest in the Indian real estate either you can wait for some time or be aware that you have sufficient reason available to negotiate better on the prices.

Pitfalls in Indian Real estate sector

So after going through the above chapters on retail and real estate, I am sure you can easily see that real estate sector is overly hyped and prices are unreasonable. So now you could be ready to negotiate better in India.

However, before going further it would be good for you to know some of the hype and other pitfalls in Indian real estate sector. Let's have a look at them;

Let's have a look at various arguments which has been used to sell Indian property market to investors in the UK seminars and other hype predicted by world leading companies and associated pitfalls.

(1) 300 million middle class people living in India by 2010 (higher than the US)

The only people who are using this argument to sell the Indian property market are the one who have never been to India and lived there.

Pitfalls: I have already highlighted in the previous chapters "myth about 300 million Indian" that there is no comparison of Indian and US market and Indian market is nowhere as strong as the US market.

The simple fact that *only* 31.5 million Indian (officially) earn over about £1250 **per years** (FY 2007) is enough to prove that there is no such 300 million Indian middle class higher than the US(in income terms).

(2)Huge Demand for Housing

Argument in favour of high demand of housing complex in India is that the demand for property is so high that the market is struggling to meet supply.

It is highlighted that *strong economic growth in India and a growing middle class will help fuel a huge demand for property and there is a shortfall in the residential sector at approximately 20 million units according to Indian government official figures.*

Pitfalls: *Above statement is misleading.* It does not clarify on which budget middle class Indians are looking for their housing needs and on what price there is a huge demand in India.

I agree that it is true that there is a huge shortage of quality budget homes for the middle class income group and there will always be a big housing demand considering the size of Indian population but the point is at what price?

If you look at the budget which a normal Indian middle class would be happy to spend, it is not the one which builders in India are interested in or have built the houses in the past, because of very low profit margins.

Recently MagicBricks.com an India's leading property site conducted an online survey. The survey has received over 1,000 responses from Indian netizens.

Commenting on the MagicBricks.com survey findings, Mr. R. Sundar, CEO, Times Business Solutions remarked, "*a 2-bedroom home within 5-10 lakhs (between £6500 to £ 12500 UK pounds) is the aspiration of the average Indian, who dreams of his own roof over his head."*[59].

"The survey finds that more than 50% of Indians online are looking for a 2-bedroom house to call their home, and find the Rs 5-10 lakh bracket affordable. Of this, about 54 per cent users belonged to the megacities of Delhi, Mumbai, Chennai, Bangalore, Hyderabad and Kolkata .The remaining 46 per cent came from smaller cities and towns like Nasik, Ludhiana, Batala, etc"[59].

Now to be honest this survey results even surprised me. As of my own perception, affordable flats in the bracket of Rs 10 lakh to Rs 25 lakh (between £12,500 to £30,000 UK pounds) can be sold easily in mega cities like Delhi, Mumbai, Chennai, Bangalore, Hyderabad and Kolkata for middle class Indians and in small cities the range between 5 to 10 lakh (between £6500 to £12500) is easily saleable; if target customer are middle class Indians and I am sure with in this range millions of unit can be sold in India.

However, if you look at the prices at which builders and developers are offering the flats in Indian cities, you might get a shock: Let's have a look:

> **Hampton International (UK) is offering apartments in Gurgoan city in India from minimum GBP £125,000 (quarter million dollar minimum).**

> **For 4 bed room flats prices start from** £234,000, (almost half a million dollar).

Companies like Navyroof.com Ltd. (UK) an independent property investment company in the UK are doing number of free seminars and offering property in a place called Rudrapur (a very small town) in Uttaranchal state in India.

Two bed apartments - from £35,325

Three bed room apartments from **£43,885**

This is the price at which they are offering properties in the small town for Western investor when the property pricing in India are crashing and where Indian middle class people are looking for buying 2 bedroom apartments in the range of *between £6500 to £ 12500 UK. How the investor would earn the profit?*

The point which property investment companies in the UK are making to investors is that property prices are falling in the UK and India is coming up, and there is already an appreciation of 70% in last year and according to Merrill Lynch there would be 700% growth in from 2005 to 2015 and so on…

So every investor would be looking forward for this opportunity especially the ones who have extra surplus funds and after having heard a lot of hype about Indian market £40000 to £50000 is not a big sum of money.

Now do you think foreign investors would get good appreciation in India if he purchases the property at £35,325 in a small town where Indians are willing to pay only up to £12500 for the similar property???

Do you think that there would be very big appreciation for foreign investor at these prices when property prices are crashing???

One gets a good appreciation when one purchase property at less price and sell at high price. **Now these builders and developers are already selling these properties at very high prices,** which even higher income group Indians will not buy at this price in small town.

Why would any *Indian go to this small town and live there where there are hardly any amenities as compared to any mega city?*

Why wouldn't any Indian prefer to buy the property in mega city at this price?

Do you know when the foreign investor will get the appreciation on these properties???

It will be *only* when another foreign investor will also be mislead and buy the hype around this property from the first foreign investor hoping that he can get good appreciation as India is coming up.

Now do you know who will make the maximum profit out of this whole game?

The property investment companies in the UK. You would not have time to go to India for one property which is not even ready right now. So they will manage the property for you and there will be a charge for that.

They can fully furnish the flat for you however there would be extra exorbitant charge for you.

They can do all the legal work for you and there would be extra charge for you.

There will be coterie of local builders, local agents and local lawyers who will also be sharing the profits.

Last but not the least the local resident who would have never thought of making such huge money in short time. Their property price would appreciate which would be paid by foreign investor sitting in Manchester or London.

The investor would be kept waiting for number of years for profits to come and of course even if you lose the money, chances are that you don't tell other people as nobody wants to look stupid in front of others.

So I want to summarise my point here:

Yes there is very huge demand for housing in India as per government official estimate *but only in the price category which is not very profitable for foreign investor considering the time and efforts it involves.*

(3) 7 fold increase predicted in value of the property market from 2005-2015 (Merrill Lynch)

If the foreign investors keep on speculating in Indian market and massive flow of investment keep on continue in the real estate sector for the next 7 years then may be at some place in India only but still not everywhere.

For prices to go up 700% you need people whose income are also going up consistently and the end users to support that price which is not the case, as Indian salaries which saw astronomical rise for many years has started stagnating (as they already reached very high level) and Indian middle class end users is not willing to pay what builders and property investment firms are asking.

Also it is interesting to see that the Merrill lynch which has predicted 700% increase in Indian property market, itself has lost $ 7.8 Billion dollars in US property market in 2007.

"Wall Street banking giant Merrill Lynch has unveiled a huge loss for 2007, crippled by exposure to risky investments in the US housing market. It made a net loss of $7.8bn (£3.9bn) in the 12 months to the end of December 2007".[60]

(4)Fraud and crime

Unfortunately, the Indian real estate sector still lacks professionalism and is still under the grip of local politicians and goons. This is one business which has seen people becoming millionaire overnight i.e. attract all kind of scrupulous people in this business.

Because of the presence of all kind of scrupulous people maximum fraud is done by property agents and builders in the country which often leads to physical attack and in some cases even murders.

There are various kinds of tricks which are used by dubious developers and agents in India. Let's have a look at some of them.

One of the common frauds done by developers is to pay little advance to the main land owners while purchasing land for development and then show the receipt as proof of the land transfer to the public for selling plots.

The fraud here is that the developers do not own the whole land as he has only paid the little advance but has already started selling the land and there could be the possibility that after collecting huge money he may run away.

Another possible scam is that even though some of the realtors have purchased all of the land but that does not mean that the layout of plot is approved by the government authorities to sell to the public and it is always the consumer who normally ended up suffering.

Not only that, sometime developers claim that their project has been approved by respective development authority (Govt body) but that does not mean that the approval has actually been obtained.

Thousands of such cases are lying pending with the various state consumer redressel commission in India. If you're thinking that these scams may be done only in small cities or by small developers then think again.

Recently in year 2007, a millions dollar scam was unearthed in Delhi, capital of India. *"Multi-crore scam in real estate unearthed"*[61].

According to news published on the The Hindu," *A multi-crore scam in real estate has been unearthed by the Economic Offences Wing of the Delhi police with the arrest of a promoter of Rajshree Group who allegedly floated real estate entities and cheated over 600 investors"[53]...." The brochure projected Rajshree Group as an Indo-Swedish joint venture. The company was shown as one of the fastest growing real estate developers in the National Capital Region; whereas it had no history of any real estate development projects"[53]..." More than 600 investors fell prey to the hype created by the company and invested over Rs. 13 crore (3.25 million dollar)"[61].*

Scam on agricultural land...

Another common scam is where agricultural land is sold for non-agricultural purposes without land conversion.

As a rule, non-agriculturists cannot purchase farmland. However this rule is also frequently violated by registering agricultural lands in favour of non-agriculturists.

Agricultural land which is available for very cheap prices is split into smaller blocks and sold separately for commercial purpose (at high prices) without land conversion. *Many times in these scams, government officers like sub-registrars or registrar are also involved* which make very difficult for an ordinary investor to detect the fraud.

In fact not only people at registrar level are involved in property scams but even some times chief ministers of the states are also involved in various kind of scams in India. *"Chargesheet against Punjab ex-CM (chief minister) in real estate scam"[62].*

What can a common man do when the people who are ruling and running the government itself are involved in the scams???

Same plot (land) sold to many people…

Another scam practices by property agents in India is to sell the same plots to different people, which leads to violence and sometimes even murders.

Recently in March 2008, a Delhi police (ACP) Assistant Commissioner of Police was shot dead in a property disputes in Gurgaon city (Near Delhi).

This ACP was not an ordinary Delhi police officer rather more like a "Dirty Harry" better known as "encounter specialist".

This gentleman has worked a lot to clean up the country from various terrorist and criminals. So far he has killed 56 terrorists in the country and in fact was a terror for the criminals and terrorist.

Many murders have taken place after that incident however the reason I want to choose this incident is just to highlight the audacity of people in property trade that they even didn't hesitate to attack on a person of his calibre who was the only police officer who was provided **Z+** security (*which has a security cover of 36 personnel*) and only available to people of cabinet minister and Prime minister level.

The profession of property agents does not leave a good impression in the mind of Indian people as most of the people who enter into this profession are uneducated and rough. It would be rare to find property agents in India who are well polished and properly educated (*The only exception may be staff in the MNC which are entering in the Indian real estate sector).*

As most property agents are uneducated and rough, violence and crime is not something they are really afraid of especially when big money is involved and the country legal system is too slow.

There are variety of property scams in India and one needs to be careful while buying any property or dealing with estate agents in India.

Quality of life promised in media advertisements...

Another Pitfall in Indian Real estate sector is the **quality of life** which is normally promised in big advertisements by even most respected developers is hardly matched in reality.

The fact is that they highlight only partial facts and not the whole picture. It is the end user who suffers in the end, if he/she does not properly investigate before investing.

Sometimes it is not only the Indian agents who create hype about properties but even the International companies do the same in India.

Let's have a look at the following advertisement about property.

Palm Drive, Gurgaon (India)

XYZ is delighted to present Garden Terraces at The Palm Drive, Gurgaon. These low rise residences present a new standard in luxury living.

• Two apartments on each floor...• Two and a half acres of communal garden...

Prices start from £234,000 for four bedroom apartments...

Palm Drive is a development ...in the green pastoral settings of Gurgaon, one of the commercial hubs of the National Capital Region. Spread across 37.8 acres of land…

The development as a whole will comply with **international standard specifications** and will have a wide range of amenities including: • Golf course • Club house • Swimming pool • World class gymnasium • Tennis court • Jacuzzi• Multi-purpose function hall…contact us today for more information.

This advert is by the company, which currently has an international network of over 85 offices worldwide, with its headquarters based in the prestigious place, Grosvenor Square, London (UK).

This is also considered as one of the most respected residential agency in the UK and is marketing properties in the Gurgaon city in India.

There is nothing wrong in the advert except that it does not give a complete picture about the quality of life especially if you are considering buying a **holiday** home in India.

Apart from the fact that the property is at very high price as per Indian market standard, the main point here is that private developers develop their own complexes only but *civic utilities like roads, water, electricity, sewer and transport are falling apart* in this city of Gurgaon and the whole situation is never mentioned to the buyers.

When an investor invests his or her money, he or she also wants peace of mind apart from the flat/house specifications. Marketing agency will let you know about everything that is inside the complex and gives the impression that the living standards are parallel with International living standards, however reality is far from it, the moment you come out of the complex.

Could you believe that in this city where apartments are sold, giving the impression of International living standards has the following:

(a) The roads which are full of potholes.

(b) Some of the area in the city where electricity cut for 12 hours a day (unheard in the UK or the US).

(c) No proper public transportation system.

(d) Every second day there are incidence of burglary and crime.

(e) Traffic is completely chaotic and jams are usual features.

(f) Air and noise pollution.

Residents are assured of 24 hours electricity by the developers and that is true but the fact is that supply is only for 12 hours a day for many months from the state government side and during those months electricity is generated by the generators which create noise and at the same time pollution which is never mentioned.

Well, city of Gurgoan has all the above issues which make the life really stressful for the residents. I don't think that anyone would like to make a big investment to live in a city to lose his/her peace of mind because of the fear of high crime rate but these points are never mentioned in those adverts.

Gurgoan is a city where offices of all the multinational companies are operating and once advertised as perfectly planned city with International standards, is really in a pathetic state now on various parameters.

The city has been mushrooming with high rise apartment that promises everything from full power backup to tennis courts, swimming pools, spas.

There are plenty of shopping malls and glittering high rise offices and building of multinational organizations but *all against the backdrop of traffic jams, potholed roads, chaotic Infrastructure growth and high rate of crime.*

There have been so many malls come up in the city one after another, that traffic and the parking situation at the moment has become totally chaotic and not to mention that many of those shopping malls are also failing which were sold on big hype. *However the developers who sold them maintain that malls are not well-researched and some just don't have the correct mix of retail format.*

Property Scams:

(a)Some developers and agents sell the same piece of land or apartments to several customers.

(b) There are developers who sell land without clear titles.

© There has been instances of construction by builders without permissions from the government authorities, violating building by-laws and they sell these apartments to normal public which suffers later on as builders have already run away once they take the money.

(d) Agriculture land is sold for non-agricultural purposes without land conversion.

(e) Claim in various advertisements that such and such project has been approved by respective development authority (Govt body) could also be false.

(f) Developers started selling the land without owning it and there could be the possibility that after collecting huge money he may run away.

(g) Some of the projects in unorganized sector do not have even government permission to build.

(h) Artificial hype is most often created while selling. **Quality of life** which is normally promised in big advertisements by even most respected developers is hardly matched in reality.

Dealing with Property Agents in India

Property agents in India are excellent psychologist, *of course without any university degree.*

Often change their own statements so you need to be alert all the time when dealing with them.

You cannot take anything on face value or on their words, always insist to have everything in writing.

Before making any payments always cross -check with the respective, government land departments, about the actual fact which property agents has explained to you.

Point to remember:

 (1) This is one area which is not regulated and opaque in India.

(2)Properties are massively undervalued on the paper 100 % to 200 % or may be much more in some cases and a big amount of black money is invested in properties in India. (*Exceptions are when government itself is selling the flats or the big developers of national level are involved).*

(3) Number of Income Tax assesses in India are still very small. This suggests that the numbers of the Indian middle class was grossly overestimated. Affordability has to be key criteria in India. The correction in price is unavoidable in all the projects launched at prices which the salaried middle class Indian cannot afford.

(4) Excessive price rise in Indian property prices has cooled down the demand. It is reflected by a decrease in property registrations in major cities of India. I believe that overall prices in property market will stagnate or will decline 10 to 20 per cent in the next one year across all the main Indian cities.

(5) *One word of advice* not to buy a new premium apartment, as there are plenty available for re-sale in the similar category which could be 20 to 40 per cent cheaper depending upon your negotiation skills as speculators are moving out and end-users are buying cautiously.

I think greater transparency and a dedicated regulator to address the consumers concern and complaints is a must in the Indian property market.

Education System

India is perceived in the West as a country of the largest English speaking skilled workforce, who are technology savvy and hard working, which is true. This is also one of the reasons why the biggest companies in the world are shifting their research and development centres to India. However there are number of pitfalls in the education system of our country. Let's have a look at them.

Professional courses are hardly practical and updated

If you look at course curriculum for Engineering and Management courses in India, you might feel surprised that most of the professional courses in most universities emphasise largely on the *theoretical aspect* of the course only and are rarely *updated*.

Professional courses in India do have the practical hours in it **but the point is *they are very few* and they do not prepare the graduate to face the market when he come out**.

You could take any fresh civil engineering graduate in India who has just completed his exams and put him on the construction site, I bet he wouldn't have a clue and cannot handle the project unless given practical training for a couple of months. **So what is the point of spending 4 years in engineering college with only theory when the engineering graduate is not employable?**

Theoretical course structure of professional courses in India put enormous pressure on the industry to train them again so they can be of practical use. It results in national wastage of millions of hours.

Professional courses in India need to be practical and updated.

Substandard universities and education system

It is only at some of India's renowned universities where the education system is on par with the international level.

In most universities, the education standard is far below than what it should be. This affects the quality of students who graduate from them. Majority of students who passed out of Indian universities are not employable by the Indian Industry.

This is not only my view but even confederation of Indian Industry (CII) feels the same. "Only *39.5 per cent of graduates in India are employable and the challenge is to bridge the human resources gap by providing skills training to the other 60 per cent, says a Confederation of Indian Industry-Aspire report released at the 'Skills World 2008' summit organised by the CII and Aspire*".[63]

Faculty in Business schools in India

During my own management studies and while teaching as guest professor in various MBA colleges in India, I was shocked to find out that most of the faculties that are teaching business studies to students have never done the business in their own life.

Usually the faculty members are those who have completed simple MBA degree and start teaching and some even without any management qualification.

How come a person who has never been in corporate sector and has never done the business can teach about the business?

But this is what is happening in most of the Indian Business schools.

Associated Chambers of Commerce and Industry of India **(ASSOCHAM) has revealed a shocking statistic about the knowledge base of faculty members of Indian MBA schools.**

"Barring the top 30, faculty in most business schools in the country lack fundamental economic awareness, says a study conducted by the Associated Chambers of Commerce and Industry of India (ASSOCHAM)".[64]

"The ASSOCHAM Business Barometer (ABB) survey on faculty awareness covered 258 faculty members in various MBA institutes across the country – except the top 30 – and discovered that **89 per cent of the teachers didn't know the GDP growth rate in financial year 2006-07"**.[64]

Isn't it is shocking?

"Not even 10 percent of the teachers were aware of the existing financial turmoil in the US". [64]

"As many as 91 per cent of the lecturers teaching business environment did not know how to read budget papers. ...The survey further divulged that hardly 6 percent of the lecturers surveyed read any business newspaper on regular basis. Moreover, persistent readers of business magazines were negligible".[64]

"Most of the case studies or examples discussed in the class are outdated, as faculties use old editions". [64]

Now if the business school teachers themselves are ill-informed, then what knowledge they would deliver to the students?

This means majority of management students in India are barely graduating without any proper knowledge and experience, so what contribution they would make to the country, multinational organizations and particularly to the consulting organizations who create a big hype?

Unlike the West, **even in top 30 MBA schools in India percentage of fresh graduate (without any industry experience) who directly enter into business schools is very high**.

I think if students have even one year work experience in the industry and then come to study in business schools it would make more sense rather than without any experience coming fresh to business schools.

All what they get is bookish knowledge of management and a good vocabulary from the professors who have never done the business in their own life.

If this is the condition of graduates from top 30 business schools in India then what about the rest of B schools graduate?

If you think what you have read above is shocking then keep on reading further as you are about to get a bigger shock from Government of India initiatives on degrading the quality of whole of skilled work force in India because of vote bank politics.

Quotas system in Government education institutions including the top ones...

Divide and rule has always been a good strategy for rulers in India (whether Indians or not) from centuries and it works well.

Despite the facts we (Indians) tell the world that we are one and living happily together but deep inside, the minds of the people is still divided on the basis of caste at least in those areas where people are illiterate and this is the reason that in India, politics based on caste system still works.

Now the political parties in India understand this very well. Decades ago, one of the ruling parties introduced the quota system in government educational institutes for one caste to please them and to win the votes. Initially this was introduced for 10 years and the "idea" was that people from these castes are poor and that they have low representation in government jobs and educational institutions and by giving reservations their living standard could be improved.

After 10 years it was extended for another 10 years and so on and it was never abolished, rather to gain more and more votes, political parties keep on extending to include other caste as well.

Now the drawback in this policy is that here **various ruling parties consciously tried to divide the people** of India in the name of caste by favouring one section of society.

If the intentions of political parties are really genuine to help the poor people, then this quota or reservation should have been based on economical criteria rather than caste so all the poor people irrespective of any caste could have been benefited but that didn't happened.

Not only that the whole concept of quota and reservation system is flawed in itself and will be encouraging mediocrity in Indian skilled workforce and would have negative effect on growth and development of one section of society who got the reservation.

By giving quota to one section of society, political parties are telling them subconsciously that you are inferior and you don't have to work hard as we have reserved the seats for you (*making them less competitive and less hardworking*).

Let's see why. For example in any education institution considering there are 100 seats and if there is 25 % quota for a particular caste.

Let's say there is an open competition for getting into the education institution. So now there will be 2 admission lists because of quota system, one for general category and other for students from one caste for whom seats are reserved.

In general candidate list let's say there could be a cut off list of marks, say at 80 % marks and in reserved caste category cut of list of marks could be hardly at 30 % marks.

So student in general category at 79% marks could not get admission even though poor but candidates in quota category from particular caste even 31 % marks can get the admission even though he or she may be rich.

So the quality of people who would come out of even top institute of India would not be the best.

Now to make the matter worse **recently** on recommendation of Central government *"The Supreme Court upheld 27 per cent reservations for the OBCs in central educational institutions"*.[65]

"The new policy, if implemented, would take the overall reservation in the Government-funded higher education institutions from the current 22.5 per cent (for SC and ST students) to 49.5 per cent".[65]

So that means almost 50 % of graduate even from the top Indian institute like IIM (Management), AIIMS (Medical) and IIT (Engineering), and all other government institution would be the one who are just mediocre.

"The Centre's main plank was that OBCs (other backward categories), who have been oppressed for centuries, needed a helping hand by means of quota and that caste was an accepted form of determination of backwardness as it was the basis for oppression and resultant backwardness".[65]

If various political parties in India really want to unite people and want to lift the living standard of poor people, the best solution would have been the NO QUOTA SYSTEM at the first place.

The criteria for admission to educational institutions should be based strictly on merit rather than caste or even poverty.

But at the same time to help the poor people all kind of extra facilities should be provided so that people who want to rise up but are economically weak should not be at disadvantageous position.

There could be provisions of (a) free career counselling and seminars to create awareness (b) free coaching scheme (c) free competitive exams books for poor people (d) No admission fee for educational institutions (e) No competitive entrance exam fees, etc.

There could be number of other ideas which could be generated to help economically weak students.

So in this way the quality of people who complete their education from educational institute would be maintained and at the same time people who are economically weak would be motivated to work hard and would feel proud that they have entered the top institute on their own.

To make the matter worse for the Industry, the government of India is planning reservation of jobs in the private sector as well on the basis of caste.

That means if implemented, all the private companies in India including multinational organization will be forced to employ people from a category / caste who are considered under-privileged and it does not matter whether they are fit for the jobs or not.

This system of job reservation is already working in Government jobs and now government is planning to introduce it in private sector as well.

"The job quota in the private sector would mean reversing the clock to the 'licence-permit-quota raj' days, the FICCI Secretary General said".[66]

According to Mr Amit Mitra, Secretary General of the Federation of Indian Chambers of Commerce and Industry (FICCI) *"The minute you provide reservation on a caste, creed or religion basis, it will be incompatible to global competitive HR policy,"*.[66]

However this has not been implemented yet, but if implemented, it could be a serious problem for all the multinational organizations which are operating in India and employing Indian workforce.

BPO & IT Industry

The growth of BPO industry was phenomenal in India during 2001 to 2007, perhaps fastest in the world. Work and Jobs were outsourced to India from all over the world and in business circle people started calling India as back office of the world.

Not only that most of the big companies including Microsoft, IBM, Intel, Google, Yahoo and Cisco have opened their research and development centres in India to tap India's low-cost and vast engineering talent pool to make products and offer services to the world markets.

The primary reason for massive growth and profit margins of domestic BPO and IT companies was profitable business model; Earning in dollars and pound and payment to their Indian employees in rupees.

This revenue models worked well in India for years however now the BPO and IT industry in India is also threatened because of following reasons;

(1)**Rising salary**: Salary increase in India was perhaps the fastest in the world over these years.

As hundreds of foreign companies entered into Indian market, there was literally a war between the companies to attract the best talents and hence rising salary for the employees.

The salaries have reached such a level in India that *"Country's two largest software exporters, Infosys Technologies and Wipro Technologies, anticipate wage pressures might not* *only slash their margins but also prevent them from maintaining their **competitive advantage**."[67]*

Not only that *"Wipro has also cited wage pressure as a **business risk** in its latest annual filing to the SEC".[67]*

According to a recent survey by *"Global management consultancy firm Hay Group said salaries in India are forecast to rise by 14.4 per cent during 2008".[67]*

"Some companies witnessed a 20 per cent rise last year in the cost of running their research and development operations in India," Zinnov chief executive Pari Natarajan said in an interview". .."If this trend continues, the cost advantage of doing research and development in India compared to the US will go away," he said, predicting a shakeout in the research and development off shoring market.[68]

(2)US slowdown

The major portion of revenue of all the big Indian IT companies are driving from the US and with the slowdown in the US economy, the BPO and IT companies are also feeling the heat.

This is one of the major reasons that the growth rate of Indian IT companies have drastically reduced.

"In the three months ending in March 2008, Mumbai-based TCS reported its worst quarter since its public listing in 2005, while guidance from rival Infosys Technologies indicates this quarter will be one of the Bangalore-based group's slowest in eight years".[69]

"TCS, Infosys, Wipro, Satyam witness sharp slowdown"..."The top four IT exporters including TCS, Infosys, Wipro and Satyam that reported results for the financial year ended March 2008 have witnessed a sharp slowdown in growth. At the aggregate level, sales grew by 26% in FY08 whereas net profit (PAT) rose by 18.8%. This is much slower compared to the jump of 45.3% and 46.4% in sales and PAT, respectively, during FY07".[70]

(3) Talent crunch and very high rentals

As I have explained in previous topics on real estate that rental in Indian majors cities has already reached such a level where they are no longer practical for many organizations to operate.

High rental value in major Indian cities are forcing the companies to relocate to smaller cities to make the project workable however there are other problems associated with smaller cities. While rental may be lower but the infrastructure is almost bleeding.

Along with the infrastructure issue there is huge shortage of quality manpower in India. Despite the fact India produces one of the largest technical people in the world but unfortunately the quality of skilled people is well below the international standard.

"Only 39.5 per cent of graduates in India are employable and the challenge is to bridge the human resources gap by providing skills training to the other 60 per cent, says a Confederation of Indian Industry-Aspire report released at the 'Skills World 2008' summit organised by the CII and Aspire".[63]

According to Zinnov chief executive Pari Natarajan, "*India turns out more than half a million engineers every year, but institutions do not train them in basic research, limiting the available talent pool to no more than 100,000 people*". ..."**It's almost impossible to hire unless you compromise on the quality of talent**".[68]

Indian companies have already realised that, it was beneficial for them initially as they have attained the leverage on the basis of Indian low cost base but now it is no longer viable to further expand and operate *only* from India because of various issues involved i.e. they started opening offices and centres outside India and started hiring in foreign countries.

"Indian Infosys recruits in the UK"..."*companies are struggling to find skilled professionals at home to keep their businesses growing so now they are turning their focus overseas*".[71]

"Indian BPO to offer 800 jobs in Ireland"..."*Indian BPO major First source has spread cheer by announcing plans to create more than 800 jobs in Northern Island*".[72]

"Wipro opens centre in Malaysia"... "*Leading IT firm Wipro Ltd ...opened its global service management centre in Malaysia to cater to infrastructure and application management service requirements of customers across the Asean region through a remote service delivery model*".[73]

You may get surprised if you think that only the big Indian IT companies are moving outside India, because even small and medium size companies are trying to move out of India.

For example small companies like Blueshift with a turnover of only £1 million are looking forward to neighbouring country like Malaysia or Singapore where they believe the operating cost could be cheaper. *"The corporate tax regime in this country is a tough 33% whereas when I look at neighbouring country Singapore it is only 18% at the highest level,"* says Blueshift's chairman Sankaran P Raghunathan. [74]

Entrepreneur Sanjoy Bose relocated his company Buzznet labs from Chennai in India to Malaysia 3 years ago..Mr Bose believes that the move has helped him...The operating costs in Malaysia are lower than what I paid in Chennai, ...in terms of rentals, deposits and utility charges.[74]

(4)Currency Fluctuation

Appreciating rupee against the dollar is further cutting down the profit margins of most of BPO and IT companies in India.

Reasons why most of the small and medium size project may fail if outsourced to India

In my own business experience and analysis, at the moment and in the future in India unless the project which is outsourced to India is really big enough and on long term basis, it is going to be a loss making venture.

Let's see the various reasons which could result in losses by outsourcing to India.

(1)Unless the project is big enough and long term, it does not justify the time and cost of selecting a vendor in India, as normally it takes between three to twelve months to completely hand the work over to an offshore partner.

(2)You need to make provision for laying off the staff in your own organization in your home country which will also lower down the morale of staff and could lower down the productivity in your own parent organization.

(3) There will be a cost to manage the contract.

(4)There is an additional cost of training because of cultural differences in Indian and Western management style.

(5)Biggest drawback is bleeding infrastructure which is major drawback. It is very difficult to imagine how things work in India if you have only lived in the UK or US.

(6) High employee attrition rate in India.

(7) Perhaps the fastest salary increases in the world which makes it very difficult to justify the savings by outsourcing.

(8) Extremely slow and inefficient legal system, which makes it almost impossible to claim any damage if your partner or vendor in India didn't deliver as per the contract.

In fact nowadays there are fewer companies in comparison to earlier years, who are looking towards India as a favoured low cost outsourcing destination because of other emerging other low cost countries.

"Focused on UK's top IT service providers, a study by Pierre Audoin Consultants (PAC) showed that China, Morocco and Hungary are the new locations of choice to set up offshore sourcing centres".[75]

"According to the study, since the beginning of January 2007, UK's 20 largest IT services suppliers have opened 21 new global delivery centres. However, of these only two are were located in India".[75]

Many companies are even looking forward and planning to close their Indian operations.

"British insurance major Aviva, which is one of the major firms outsourcing work to India, is considering selling two of its four companies in the South Asian country".[76]

"Travelport Group, the travel-services business owned by buyout group Blackstone, sold its Indian back-office operation, to Intelenet Global Services Pvt Ltd, a Mumbai-based company, according to sources".[76]

"Smarting under mounting costs and employee attrition, about 15% of captive units of multinational parents are working on an exit strategy that could include a partial or full exit, says a latest report by Forrester Research on firms in IT and product development work".[77]

"Unable to find cost savings from their Indian captive centres, some firms have chosen to believe that the problem is India itself and decide to try another location".[77]

"Lehman has decided to drop its plans for a back-office unit in Delhi. The proposed unit, designed as a support centre for market-related investment services, was scheduled to open in the last week of March. Lehman is also shutting down its mortgage capital division in India, where it employs over 100 people".[78]

"JP Morgan has closed its equity research operation in India".[78]

"Citigroup is in the process of selling its Indian back-office operations, where it employs over 5,000 people".[78]

Now when even big companies are struggling to justify the cost savings and planning to close down their back office operations in India, interesting news is that even now in 2008 many companies in the UK and the US are luring small and medium size entrepreneurs by organizing seminars about business opportunities in India, so they can invest in India or to outsource to India to get benefits.

Banking services in India

The Banking system is fairly efficient in India, particularly in the private banks like Standard Charted, HDFC, etc compared to that in the UK.

Business people from the UK would be surprised to find out that the banking system is much faster and more efficient in India.

Normally it takes about 5 days to clear a cheque in the UK while the same may be cleared in India in usually 2 days.

Online funds transfer takes about 3 days in the UK while the same would be done instantly in India.

For opening a bank account you may need to take appointment in the UK which may take anywhere between one to three weeks, while in India your bank account can be opened on the same day within half an hour, just walk in any bank.

Banking system, in the private bank, is very efficient in India as compared to that in the UK.

Telecommunication services in India

I must say that the way private Indian telecommunication companies are working in India is really amazing. Here I am comparing Indian private sector telephone companies to British Telecom in the UK.

I remember that in around year 2002 in New Delhi, I ordered fixed telephone line connection from one Indian leading private telephone company.

I was given a tentative time period of 7 days in which my landline connection would be installed and all the wiring would be done. However the whole job was done within 3 days to my surprise.

In year 2005, I requested a telephone connection from British Telecom in London.

I was given 21 days time, which only after my persistent following up come down to about 14 days.

I would also say that telephonic services both landline and mobile are not only efficient but also economical in India.

In India you don't have to wait for half an hour before hearing any voice from customer support and also you don't have to pay extra for calling any customer support line because this is what companies are supposed to provide at the minimum.

Telecommunication services in the private sectors are very efficient in India as compared to that in the UK.

On the parameter of **enforcing contract**, *India ranked embarrassingly low at 177 out of 178 world economy*. Even West bank and Gaza were ranked at 125, well above India. China rank impressively at 20 in comparison to India.

Source: Doing business 2008 (World Bank)

Legal System in India

Although the point of carefully drafting the contract cannot be overemphasised, however, there are some other important points about Indian legal system which you must be aware of while doing business in India.

(1) Indian legal system is *too... slow*. (Millions of case are pending in Indian court and it take years to get justice, sometime 10 years or it could be 20 years or may be more).

(2) Indian courts don't award the compensation anywhere near to the kind of one being awarded in Europe or especially in US.

Now because of the above two main reasons, businesses and the people in India have little faith in Indian judiciary system and crimes in general and forgeries in businesses are rising like anything.

Scrupulous businessmen in India understand this very well and don't mind cheating if they need to. Now you need to be aware of the fact to avoid costly mistake that *contracts doesn't mean everything in India. Signing a contract in India doesn't mean that it will be honoured word by word* as there are numerous incidents where contracts in businesses were not honoured in India.

Not all businesses are unreliable in India but unlike in the West where the contract is the final word on a business deal, Indians approach to a business contract is more relaxed.

Another important point you need to be careful about before setting any project in India is about differences in Indian central government and state government interest. The ruling party which is ruling in the central government may not be the same in various other small states in India and there could be a possibility that it may affect your project. Let's see how:

For example let's say you are setting up a project in one of the state in India which needs central government approval and let's say that it has been approved by the central government, however, if in that state the ruling party is not the same as in the centre, there could still be a possibility that your project may get held up because state government ruling party may oppose the central government decision. So you need to be aware of this fact from the beginning.

Point to remember: *Check* the background of Indian vendor, (**selecting the right vendor** *is the best safeguard in my understanding*)their systems, capability of management team, if they have done the similar project as yours in the past and if possible do have a word with their one or two of their client & preferably deal with the already established organization.

It is good to start with small project initially to see how the vendor provides the services and how much willing to accommodate.

Unwritten agreements are best to be avoided in India. Keep an eye on new rules and regulations.

How Indian companies stay competitive?

Well, no magic mantra for staying competitive except that Indian companies make sure the cost of operation is reduced at every front and they keep inventing.

Following two examples can throw more light on the way Indian companies operate and save money.

(1)First example is from India's second largest IT company;

"In a bid to curtail its training expenses (which rose to $170 million, this year) and shorten time to billing for new joinees, India's second largest IT company Infosys is now hiring engineering students whilst in their third year and putting them on internship for 17 weeks. This way the company saves on the three months salary, which it provides to its trainees and makes them billable faster when they join Infosys".[79]

"During the internship, the students get a Rs 1,000 (about £12.5 pounds) stipend from Infosys apart from free boarding and lodging".[79]

(2) Recently a movie was filmed in London and it was a joint venture between the UK production house and Indian directors who were also managing.

(a)On the film set, salary for Indian staff which was brought from India was in rupees as they would have received in India, however, on the same film set the staff from the UK were paid the salary as per the UK standard.

(b)Even the food which was purchased was different for both the Indian team and the UK one.

(c)The entire Indian team was given accommodation at least one hour distance away from London where cheap accommodation was available and most of them were accommodated there.

This way Indian side cut the cost on salary, food and accommodation.

Now I knew by now some of you would already be thinking that it is unethical.

Well, the answer is yes but if you look at it from the point of view of the Indian staff who work on film set, they were more than happy.

The reason is they normally get a salary of £100 to £200 a month in India and coming from very poor family background, they could never get the visa for London at this salary on their own in the whole of their life, let alone extra free flying experience which is a dream for them.

Anyhow my objective here is not to get into debate about what is ethical but just to explain by giving a practical example as to how Indian companies try to stay competitive.

On **dealing with licences**, India ranked at 134 out of 178, well below Mexico at 21, Tonga 30, Jamaica 74, Kenya 9, and Pakistan 93, US at 24 and the UK at 54.

Source: Doing Business 2008 (World Bank Group)

Can India sustain over 8% economic growth until 2020?

According to a report by Goldman Sachs" *India will sustain about 8 % growth until 2020 and may become the second largest economy in the world, ahead of the U.S., by 2050"*.[49]

It is interesting to observe the above statement by one of the world most respected organizations.

With due respect to the research team of Goldman Sachs who came to the above analysis, I don't think that the above analysis will come out to anywhere near reality unless speculation and investments by foreign funds continue in India for the next 10 to 12 years based on the report of Goldman Sachs and other similar reports made by various other consulting organization which may fuel further speculations and foreign investment and all the other conditions (external factors) remain ideal for so many years.

Let's have a look at some of the basic fundamentals which can effect economic growth in India.

(1)Infrastructure:

I think infrastructure in any country is the key for development and economic growth.

A well developed infrastructure in any country is similar to arteries and vein network in the healthy human body and extremely important for nation growth. *Now imagine for a second, can a human body remain healthy for long time if the network of arteries and vein network get choked?*

Of course not and that is precisely the situation of infrastructure in India at the moment, it is **choked *and getting worse*.**

Let us take a case of a city and look at the situation from various perspectives.

I am taking the example of Delhi, the capital, considering the fact that this is the city where Indian government would give maximum emphasise to provide the best of services as all the foreign diplomats, VIP lives here apart from being the seat of government.

At present sadly but truly the Delhi city is having the problems which could be associated with any overcrowded and mismanaged city.

Let me give you a feel of traffic problem in capital city Delhi, comparing it to traffic situation in London to get a better idea.

I know people *feel suffocated* in tubes and trains during peak morning and evening office hours in London. The tubes and trains are packed and certainly roads are also crowded in London.

Now imagine what will happens to London city transport if its *population* become double (*Delhi population is more than double of London population with almost same area as London city*)   +

To make matter worse Imagine with double population *only* 3 tubes of London are working. (*Delhi at the moment is running only 3 tube lines*).

Can you imagine traffic chaos in London with double the population with only 3 tube working???

Not only that imagine more than 80 % of the connecting trains are also late and ... imagine what would happen to traffic problem?

In addition to above you can add unruly private bus drivers on the road of Delhi whose buses are famous as killer blue line as these buses almost kill one person everyday.(*Buses compete with each other to get maximum passengers to maximise revenue and drive in unruly way*).

Let me put it in equation

Delhi Traffic situation = (London double population + only 3 London underground tubes working + unruly private bus drivers on road + more than 80 % connecting trains late and ... etc)

People waste everyday millions of hours just because of inefficient and overloaded road network in the major cities of India.

Some of the days, people waste half of their day only for travelling from one place to another. **The road network is getting further chocked day by day and becoming worse.**

On the top of that peoples from villages are migrating to big cities in mass numbers for employment especially in Delhi and Mumbai loading the already overloaded infrastructure.

Even in the capital Delhi, electrical cables hung from electric poles since decades ago causes major safety hazards, and power cuts are common along with voltage fluctuation. *Can you imagine daily electricity cut in London that too when it is burning with the temperature of 40 degree centigrade plus or about 105 to 110 degree Fahrenheit?*

The city's ability to deliver a regular water supply is often under pressure and quality of water supply is also substandard (admitted by Indian government itself). *Can you imagine water supply in the tap only for few hours every day in London which too is substandard?*

Imagine the city of London for moment, with double the population, only 3 tubes working, traffic jams, air and noise pollution, temperature 40 degree centigrade, electricity cut takes place every day, water supply only few hours every day which too substandard and 80 % of connecting train to city are late by an average of at least one hour.

Now imagine that *the above situation is only getting from bad to worse* and remember that this is capital city where the government takes maximum care. *Do you think any International city can run long like this with further deteriorating condition?*

This traffic, water and electricity situation is common or may be worse in all the other major cities in India. The condition of roads in small cities is pathetic.

In most of the small villages the concrete roads are still nonexistent and even don't have any access to electricity.

Do you think growth can sustain above 8% for the next 12 years in a country where most of the cities have some or the other problem as mentioned above and getting worse.

I don't understand how the continuous growth of about 8% is projected by eminent organizations when even the country capital cannot meet the most basic of human needs.

National Highways

Though the previous NDA Government led by Mr. Atal Bihari Vajpayee has taken some good step like commencing Golden Quadrilateral, a prestigious highway project, India still has a long way to go in terms of having efficient national highway in the country.

The majority of national highways in India are 2 lanes only (one in each direction).

Our national highways constitute only about 2% of the total road network in India but they handle about 40% of the total road traffic.

The condition of the majority of highways in India is nowhere as compared to the International standard.

India is losing millions of dollars due to bad quality of roads. If the roads are of bad quality, fuel consumption will be more and damages to the tyre are also more.

Not only that the safety of the people who are travelling is also in danger. Patrolling the national highways is almost non existence.

Railways

The more I would say about Indian railways the less it would be. Trains getting late in India is not unusual rather a norm.

Can you believe it that the number of **man-days lost** to **delayed trains** *in the Capital alone* **is double the number lost to all strikes in India each year.**

At least I find this news shocking!

"Train delays cause more man-hour losses than strikes"..."a random check by Times of India on a single day in Delhi shows that the number of man-days lost to delayed trains in the Capital alone is double the number lost to all strikes in India each year".[80]

"We found that more than eight out of every 10 mail or express trains that arrived at these stations on that date - midnight to midnight - were delayed".[80]

Traffic mismanagement is not the only issue, you can see mismanagement in as many areas as you may survey upon.

Ports

Low productivity and infrastructure continue to affect the performance of India's major ports.

"Longer turnaround times and evacuation of cargo still plague Indian ports, despite their efforts at modernisation of cargo handling mechanisms"..."turnaround time in major Indian ports

is about 1.77 days, as compared to 0.5 in Singapore. Similarly, the vessel evacuation rate is 40 containers per hour, compared to 100 in Singapore, while the dwell time is 3.78 days as against 0.6 in Singapore"...."Indian ports are virtually struggling to provide flawless basic infrastructure and are only equipped to provide only partial electronic data interchange services".[81]

Airports: Do you know that India has no system in place to keep strays away from airports? *"If you thought dogs, foxes and jackals holding up flights on runways was a thing of the past, here's a wake-up call...In Bangalore...the Kingfisher flight IT-2427 was obstructed by a dog on runway, breaking its nose wheel, once again raises questions about passenger safety at Indian airports". "We witness at least one incident of dog straying on runway every month,"* says an airport official in Mumbai.[82]

Finally according to U.S. chief executive officers (CEOs) *"India's poor infrastructure and bureaucratic delays as the two major irritants standing in the way of their investments in the country"*..."Unveiling the report of the US-India CEOs Forum...Forum co-Chairman William Harrison pointed out that *the lack of adequate infrastructure and the bureaucracy were the main reasons for the lack of excitement in U.S. companies about investing in India".*"I think there is lack of excitement about investing here because of factors like poor energy supply, roads, airports, ports, the core infrastructure, bureaucracy... it's hard to get approvals, permits and in the legal system, the process is slow and cumbersome and it takes a long time for settlement of disputes,"* he said.[83]

In summary I would say that condition of infrastructure is deplorable in India and I don't see any magic changes in it despite the fact billions of dollars will be invested by foreign companies in this sector. There are lots of political hurdles apart from large gestation period for foreign companies even if their projects get approved. Till the time infrastructure is not in good condition consistent impressive growth rate cannot exist in the country.

(2)Political Willingness

Our country has achieved independence more than 60 years ago but even now in years 2008, in Delhi the capital of India the water supply is substandard (admitted by government itself), so what to talk about the quality of water supply in small cities and villages in India?

Even now in New Delhi the capital of India where the all the VIP live and all the foreign dignitaries are based, 24 hour electricity is still not available.

On the top of that there is lot of voltage fluctuation which literally reduced the life of all the electrical appliances used in India.

Look at the country like Japan devastated by nuclear bomb in Second World War (nearly the same time when India got independence) has achieved phenomenal progress and then there is us after 60 years, still struggling with water and electricity supply even in the heart of India in its capital city Delhi not to mention about small cities and villages. **Can't we provide even basic water and electricity in the capital after 60 years?**

I think sure we can but what we need is political willingness without which nothing great is going to happen.

Everything flows from top to bottom. If the government is seriously willing and puts the nation's interest first I don't see any reason why things can't happen and why the country can't grow at faster rate. **But is the political willingness really there?**

(3)Population explosion

Population explosion is one thing which I understand is most detrimental to India's economic growth.

Despite extensive advertisement campaign of various successive Indian government, for creating awareness amongst the masses in India about birth control program the population in India is growing at alarming rate of growth rate of 1.38 %.

India occupies 2.4% of the world's land area and supports approx 17 % of world population (approximately one-sixth of the world's population) and it is at present 1.13 billion people (approximate estimate for March 10, 2008). Population in India is growing at an alarming rate and expected to overtake China by 2030 and will be the most populated country in the world. India's population rose by 21.34 % between 1991 – 2001.[84]

This huge population will undermine all the economic growth India may achieve in coming years and *will create numerous problems.* Problems would be ranging from food shortage, unemployment, illiteracy, crime, etc.

(4) Food shortage

First and foremost, India will be facing huge food shortage in coming years in my analysis.

From 2.4% of the world's land from where you would arrange the food for about 17% of world population??? Agricultural in India is not a profitable sector and people are shifting their profession from being a farmer or *committing suicide*.

The majority of farmers in India unlike the West have very small areas of land with primitive style farming activities. The per capita production is also very low and most of the farmers live in very poor conditions.

Everyday there are numerous reports in the media highlighting the miserable condition of farmers in India where hundreds of farmers are committing suicide in India as they can't live a self sufficient life with farming activities and mostly live under a huge debt for years and years with just enough money to survive. For example the news published on 6 Apr 2008 in The Times of India, "*9 farmers commit suicide in Vidarbha; Nine more farmers in Maharashtra's Vidarbha region have allegedly committed suicide in the first week of April, taking the total number of suicides to 255 this year*".[85]

As per news published on 30th March 2008, "*2 Amravati farmers commit suicide; Two young farmers, who had taken loans, have allegedly committed suicide at Amravati in Eastern Maharashtra*".[86]

As per another news published on 9 May 2007, *"Farmer suicide in prosperous western UP; ... As per official statistics,* **8,263 farmers have committed suicide in seven states** *(Maharashtra, Karnataka, Kerala, Andhra Pradesh, Tamil Nadu, Punjab and Gujarat) between 2003 and March 2007".*[87]

Can you imagine the plight of an Indian farmer where *in just 7 states* out of 28 states and 7 union territories of India, **8263 farmers have committed suicide** in *just 4 years* because of debt and poverty?

So what do you think what would happen to food prices in long term in India ?, obviously it would increase and in fact you would not have to wait for many years as reality is *"Retail food prices rise 40% in 4 metros; Delhi worst hit"* [88] and this price rise has happen within last one year itself.

While the small farmers are suffering in India due to extreme poverty, Indian government tried to help the farmers in a way which can appease them to win some votes for election but did not try to solve actual problem.

The Finance Minister has given Rs 60,000 crore ($15 billion) package (from tax payers money) to farmers by waving their loans.

How much of this will reach the farmers who are truly debt-stressed and mostly unaware of their right is also a serious question. But the main point is this, that it is not the way to help, rather a simple scheme to purchase the votes in the coming elections.

The loan waiver will not help the economy. By waving the loans, Finance Minister is indirectly developing the habit of farmers to not to repay the loan.

If you need to help somebody financially, the best way is to make the person independent so that he can earn himself for the whole life.

If you give money to some body without solving the real problem, the person would come to you again next year hoping he would get financial help again and in the process he would become less hardworking and more dependent.

Maybe perhaps this is what government want precisely to gain the votes but then where will be the economic growth???

Sometime I get confused when certain high dignitaries from India talk about big economic growth in India.

I don't know how can people say that India is rising or shining when in the same country about **6000 kids die every day** (2 millions kids a year) just because of hunger?

"Two million children in India die and turn into statistics every year. That's about 6,000 deaths everyday". ..."Abject poverty, lack of basic health care facilities and poor health of rural women are all killing India's under privileged, malnourished children".[89]

India is heading towards serious food shortage in coming years in my analysis and food prices will certainly be rising, considering the fact that yield per hectare is not increasing but population explosion is continuous.

This food shortage and increase in food prices will further add to increasing inflation in India or at least keep the inflation figure high.

High inflation figure will eventually bring down the economic growth.

(5) Education

Perhaps in my knowledge India may be the only country in the world where the **25 % member of the parliament has criminal case** pending against them.

"According to a recent study, the present Lok Sabha has the unique distinction of having as many as 125 members with criminal background. Serious charges of murder, rape, kidnapping, extortion and the like are pending against many of them. A media report puts their number at 139. They are all "Honourable" members. They have not been convicted yet and are not likely to be convicted in the near future,".[90]

Can you believe that in "Incredible" India, about 25 % member of the parliament have criminal background?

The elected representative reflects the thinking process of people who choose them or elect them.

How could any rational person vote for criminals? But it happens in our country.

Illiteracy along with the fear is the powerful weapon in the hand of criminal politicians, which they use to manipulate and it is not in their interest that people become educated and become more aware of their rights i.e. education projects don't get momentum in the rural area of the country.

If the poor farmers are not educated, it is difficult to transfer the new technology or knowledge to them. Illiteracy is also the root cause of many other social problems in our country. Unless the education has been given serious emphasis by government, the long term growth cannot sustain in the country.

(6) Inflation

Rising inflation is detrimental for economic growth of any country.

Inflation in India has already reached 11 % (highest in last 13 years) and I believe it will increase more and if government reduce the subsidy, it will easily shoot up to 14 percent.

Rising oil prices, (*which has already crossed $120 per barrel*), food prices and other factor are adding to inflation in India which will further undermine the growth rate in India.

(7) Employment

Everybody believes that because of economic growth in BPO, Retail and IT sector millions of jobs has been created. There is an overwhelming feeling that enough employment opportunity has been created especially for the youth.

Well, that feeling is partly true. While the number of jobs in the IT, Retail and BPO sector has certainly increased, the jobs in some of the other sector like textiles, leather, marine products and handicraft has actually decreased because of the rising rupee and decline in exports.

"The government admitted that rupee appreciation against dollar has resulted in a loss of about 20 lakh jobs (2 million jobs), besides a decline in exports".[91]

"In certain sectors like textiles, leather, marine products and handicraft, there is a net decline in exports, which has led to job losses. It was estimated that unless remedial measures are taken, the total job losses could be as high as two million," Minister of State for Commerce Jairam Ramesh informed Rajya Sabha.[91]

The high economic growth in India in the few recent years made lots of news and has become the centre point of conversation in various business seminars all over the world. Almost every single business seminar I visited in London, I could hear about the India and China economic growth reference. There was many who believe that the Indian economy has entered into a phase of high economic growth.

The question is has the Indian economy reached a stage where about 8 per cent plus growth rate can be sustained as predicted by some eminent consulting organization?

Well, at least I don't think so.

Despite the reforms, I don't see any fundamental improvement in the economy of the country that would suggest that India's can sustain above 8 percent growth.

India's economic progress seems impressive in recent years however behind this progress, is concealed an ugly reality.

Considering the example of agricultural sector which supports roughly 2/3rd of India's population or about 66 per cent of the country's population has seen only a steady decline.

India's agricultural productivity, in most cases, is one of the lowest in the world. Per capita availability of food grain is falling because of population explosion in India.

Almost nonexistent of quality rural infrastructure, most of the small villages still do not have an electricity supply or safe drinking water which adds to the woes of small farmers. India's agriculture is still highly dependent on monsoon even after 60 years of Independence & Investment in rural infrastructure is still not rising.

So what have reforms in India delivered to the nearly 66 per cent of population? Except poverty for majority of population, suicide of thousands of farmers and 6000 Indian kids dying of hunger every day. **Can we call this condition as phase of high economic growth or *"structural increase in India's potential growth rate since 2003"*[56] as Goldman Sachs report puts it?**

Government announced waiving off of agricultural loans to the extent of Rs 60,000 crore ($ 15 billion) to win the votes rather than really correcting the problem in the rural sector from the root. All the loans which are waived come from the taxpayers' pocket and not from party funds.

Growth in the country needs to be holistic and structured. Country cannot grow consistently if one segment of the society say, 1 to 2 % people get the majority of benefits of economic growth and rest of the country is lagging behind.

Subsidies are skyrocketing and the government's spending on productive areas such as infrastructure and education has been constrained by high levels of debt.

Most of the India's growth is out of touch of the real country, its villages remain as they were, rather getting poorer and neglected.

It is not possible to sustain the present economic growth of about 8 % without first making the domestic Indian markets grow at a faster pace, and that is not possible without developing rural India.

India does not seem to have gained much which would have sustained high growth. A mere five or six year long high GDP growth is seemingly choking the economy via rising inflation which has already touched 11 percent (actual figure could be more than 13 percent).

India's physical infrastructure is in deplorable state and still way behind international standards. Red-tape continues to rule the roost and corruption is rampant.

All of these add to the cost of doing business in India.

According to the latest report Doing Business 2008 (by world bank group), on the parameter of ease of doing business, *India rank 120 out of 178 world economy, below Ghana 87, Vietnam 91, Bangladesh 107, Nigeria 108, Nepal 111 and china 83.* Singapore ranked at no 1 rank, UK at rank 6 and US at rank 3. (The first place being the best. A high ranking on the ease of doing business index means the regulatory environment is conducive to the operation of business).[92]

On the parameter of enforcing contract, India ranked embarrassingly low at 177 out of 178 world economy. Even West bank and Gaza were ranked at 125, well above India. [92] *China rank impressively at 20 in comparison to India. Hong Kong at no 1 rank, Singapore at 4, the UK at 24 and US at rank 8.* (Well, this ranking on enforcing contract even surprises me. I knew that things are complicated in India but didn't realise that they are so much embarrassing).

On dealing with licences, India rank at 134 out of 178, well below Mexico at 21, Tonga 30, Jamaica 74, Kenya 9, and Pakistan 93.   St Vincent and the Grenadines at rank 1, Singapore at 5, US at 24 and the UK at 54. [92]

Now do you think a country economy can sustain its growth about 8 % per years consistently until 2020 and become the second largest economy in the world, ahead of the U.S., by 2050 with this inefficient legal system, corruption, cumbersome licensing system and choked infrastructure?

To summarise, I do not think that India has entered a higher growth path because the high growth rate over the last few years has not been structural in nature.

Without political willingness, population control, efficient legal system, proper infrastructure, higher literacy rate and increasing agriculture productivity, high economic growth cannot sustain in India and development will be limited.

Potential pitfalls while doing business in India

(1)Indian middle and upper income group, earning and spending habits are highly *overestimated* by experts from eminent consulting organization.

(2)Very high rentals / Overpriced property value

(3)Deplorable Infrastructure,

(4)Inefficient supply chains system

(5)Corruption / Bureaucracy

(6)Increasing salary / High employee attrition rate

(7)Talent crunch because of substandard education system

(8) Security threat to consumer data

(9)Training cost because of difference in Indian and Western management style

(10) Legal System is *too slow*

<u>Key facts about India</u>

Capital of India - New Delhi

Currency – Rupee (Rs)

1 Rupee = 100 paisa.

1 Lakh Rupee= One Hundred Thousand Rupee (1, 00,000) = Approx $ 2500 US Dollars or Approx £1250 UK Pounds.

1 Million Rupee = 10 Lakh Rupee = Approx $25,000 US Dollars or Approx £ 12,500 UK Pounds.

1 Crore Rupee = 10 Million Rupee or 100 Lakhs Rupee

(Considering exchange rate $1 = Rs 40 and £1 = Rs 80)

Telephone – India's country code is 91. To dial India you need to dial 00, followed by the country code 91.

Time Difference – GMT + 5.5 hours (winter)

- GMT + 4.5 hours (summer)

Electricity: 220 volts AC, 50 cycles mostly, plugs 15 amps and 5 amps with three round pins. Sockets size varies; it is advisable to have plug adaptors.

Climate: April, May, June and July are very hot *except in the hill stations*. For example the temperature in New Delhi can reach up to 45 degrees Centigrade (113 degrees Fahrenheit) in the months of June- July.

October to March is considered the best time to visit India.

Languages: Hindi is spoken in most part of north India; however, south Indians don't understand Hindi. ***English is the only language*** which is the most commonly spoken among **educated** Indians all over India. Even uneducated people can also understand commonly used words in English like thank you, sorry, etc.

English is the common language of business all over India.

National holidays in India (*Following holidays are always on fixed days every year***)**

26th January (Republic Day)

15th August (Independence Day)

2nd October (Mahatma Gandhi Birthday)

25th December (Christmas day)

140

Reference:

(1)Wikipedia the Free Encyclopedia,"Tirumala Tirupati Devasthanams: Facts"
<online> http://en.wikipedia.org/wiki/Tirumala_Tirupati_Devasthanams

(2) The Times of India, "Noida call centre in drug ring"26th March 2008 <online>
http://timesofindia.indiatimes.com/Cities/Noida_call_centre_in_drug_ring/art
icleshow/2899577.cms

(3) Best Ever Articles," Doctors steal 500 kidney in Incredible India"<online>
http://www.besteverarticles.com/blogs/4/Doctors-steal-500-kidney-in-
Incredible-India.html

(4)The times of India, "After Dr Death and Dr Kidney, Dr Greed"<online>
http://timesofindia.indiatimes.com/After_Dr_Death_and_Dr_Kidney_Dr_Gree
d/articleshow/2853934.cms

(5) NDTV, "US visa racket involving film industry unearthed"<online> March
12, 2008
http://www.ndtv.com/convergence/ndtv/story.aspx?id=NEWEN20080043843

(6)The Hindu Business Line, "4 Indians in Forbes' top 10 billionaires list"
<online>
http://www.thehindubusinessline.com/2008/03/07/stories/2008030752020100.
htm

*(7) HESA Students in Higher Education Institutions 2005/06 reveals," India now
number 2 provider of overseas students to uk"<online>
http://www.hesa.ac.uk/index.php/content/view/118/161/*

(8)U.S. Department of State, "Higher Education: A Keystone in U.S. - India
Relations"<online> http://www.state.gov/r/us/2007/82350.htm

(9) The Times of India, "Dowry death alleged" <online>
http://timesofindia.indiatimes.com/Cities/Delhi/Dowry_death_alleged/article
show/2806434.cms

(10) The Times of India, "Woman beaten up for dowry"29 Feb 2008 <online>
http://timesofindia.indiatimes.com/Cities/Woman_beaten_up_for_dowry/arti
cleshow/2824378.cms

(11) The Times of India "Man arrested for dowry harassment"<online>
http://timesofindia.indiatimes.com/Cities/Man_arrested_for_dowry_harassme
nt/articleshow/2838129.cms

(12) The Times of India, "Dowry death: Husband, in-laws detained", 24 Mar 2008
<online> http://timesofindia.indiatimes.com/Dowry_death_In-
laws_detained/articleshow/2893000.cms

(13) The Times of India, "Rajkot woman stages semi-nude protest against dowry
demand", 5 Jul 2007 <online>
http://timesofindia.indiatimes.com/articleshow/2176007.cms

(14) The Times of India, "Newborn girl found on expressway"15 Mar 2008,
<online>
http://timesofindia.indiatimes.com/Cities/Newborn_girl_found_on_expresswa
y/articleshow/2867260.cms

(15) Guardian UK, "Desperate British Asians fly to India to abort baby girls"
<online>http://www.guardian.co.uk/world/2006/jan/22/india.uk

(16) The Hindu," No girls, please, we're Indian"<online>
http://www.hinduonnet.com/mag/2004/08/29/stories/2004082900130100.htm

(17) IFES Feature Story, "Millions of Missing daughters"
<online>http://www.ifes.org/features.html?title=Millions%20of%20Missing%2
0Daughters%25IFES%20Partners%20Fight%20Sex%20Selection%20in%20India

 (18)IBN Live, Nation; "Chemical tea: Train passengers sip slow poison"<online>
http://www.ibnlive.com/news/chemical-tea-train-passengers-sip-slow-
poison/60231-3.html

(19)IBN Live, "Mumbai homemaker busts milk adulteration racket"<online>
http://www.ibnlive.com/videos/55588/mumbai-homemaker-busts-milk-
adulteration-racket.html

(20)The Times of India, "25% of milk in state adulterated" 16th June 2007
<online>
http://timesofindia.indiatimes.com/Cities/Mumbai/25_of_milk_in_state_adult
erated/articleshow/2127308.cms

(21) The Times of India, "Food adulteration goes unchecked" 21 May 2002,
<online> http://timesofindia.indiatimes.com/articleshow/13507365.cms

(22) The Times of India, Hotel owner fined in food adulteration case 7 Aug 2003, <online> http://timesofindia.indiatimes.com/articleshow/117712.cms

(23) The Times of India, "Adulteration thrives as PFA dept sits easy"21 Jul 2002 <online> http://timesofindia.indiatimes.com/articleshow/16599577.cms

(24) The Times of India," Delhi water substandard: Govt" 14 Mar 2008 <online> http://timesofindia.indiatimes.com/Cities/Delhi_water_substandard_Govt/articleshow/2863435.cms

(25) BBC News, World, South Asia, "Action needed' over Delhi smog" 14th Nov 2007 <online> http://news.bbc.co.uk/1/hi/world/south_asia/7094334.stm

(26) Meri News special, Urban Chaos, <online> http://www.merinews.com/urban_chaos.jsp

(27) Reuters Alert Net, More cars hit Delhi's anti-pollution drive - study, 21st Dec 2006 <online> http://www.alertnet.org/thenews/newsdesk/DEL238078.htm

(28) BBC News, World; "Air pollution suffocates Calcutta" 3rd May 2007 <online> http://news.bbc.co.uk/1/hi/world/south_asia/6614561.stm

(29) NDTV.com, "Forbes magazine names Mumbai as city of junk" March 6 2008 <online> http://www.ndtv.com/convergence/ndtv/story.aspx?id=NEWEN20080043169

(30) Financial Times, India-Society," Indian cities ranked last for air quality" 27th Feb 2008 <online> http://www.ft.com/cms/s/0/1d32debe-e554-11dc-9334-0000779fd2ac,dwp_uuid=0da0817c-9c86-11da-8762-0000779e2340.html

(31) The Times of India, "Indians in bigger risk of diabetes"5th March 2008 <online> http://timesofindia.indiatimes.com/Indians_in_bigger_risk_of_diabetes/articleshow/2840425.cms

(32) The Times of India, "India is world's TB capital" 19 Mar 2008 <online>http://timesofindia.indiatimes.com/India_is_worlds_TB_capital/articleshow/2879742.cms

(33) The Economics Times, "India among world's top hot spots of deadly emerging diseases", 21 Feb, 2008, <online> http://economictimes.indiatimes.com/News/News_By_Industry/Healthcare__

Biotech/India_among_worlds_top_hot_spots_of_deadly_emerging_diseases/rss
articleshow/2800737.cms

(34) Guardian UK, "Lifestyle' diseases hit India's IT workers" 14th Sept 2007
<online> http://www.guardian.co.uk/world/2007/sep/14/business.india

(35)World Bank, Finance & Development "Improving India's Saving
Performance" <online>
http://www.worldbank.org/fandd/english/0697/articles/0100697.htm

(36) Economics Times, "Indians prefer to play safe with savings" 3 Sep, 2007
<online>
http://economictimes.indiatimes.com/Personal_Finance/Savings_Centre/India
ns_prefer_to_play_safe_with_savings/rssarticleshow/2332035.cms

(37) Economics Times, "Indians prefer physical assets as savings" 8 May, 2007
<online> http://economictimes.indiatimes.com/articleshow/2015912.cms

Part 2:

(38) The Economic Times, "India has 31.5 million taxpayers" 28 Jul, 2007,
<online>
http://economictimes.indiatimes.com/India_has_315_million_taxpayers/article
show/2240281.cms

(39) Economics Times, "India drives BMW's record sales",7 Apr, 2008, <online>
http://economictimes.indiatimes.com/News_by_Industry/India_drives_BMWs
_record_sales/articleshow/2933303.cms

(40) Rediff, "India's airlines suffer Rs 4,000 cr loss in FY08",June 04, 2008,
<online> http://www.rediff.com/money/2008/jun/04airline.htm

(41) Rediff, "Airline operators set to ground 165 flights," July 05, 2008,<online>
http://www.rediff.com/money/2008/jul/05air.htm

(42) India retailing, "Retail Report" <online>
http://www.indiaretailing.com/retail-report.asp

(43) Rediff India abroad, "Mumbai: World's 4th most expensive office mart" 13th
November 2007 <online>
http://www.rediff.com/money/2007/nov/13mum.htm

(44) Daily News and Analysis, Money, "High real estate prices hit Adidas India plans" May 26, 2008 <online>
http://www.dnaindia.com/report.asp?newsid=1166595

 (45) Economics Times, "Skyrocketing land prices make restaurants go abroad" 24 Apr, 2008 <online>
http://economictimes.indiatimes.com/Skyrocketing_land_prices_make_restaurants_go_abroad/articleshow/2976955.cms

 (46)The Times of India, "Maya shutters farm retail stores of Reliance, RPG" 24 Aug 2007 <online>
http://www1.timesofindia.indiatimes.com/articleshow/2305698.cms

(47) Transparency International, Corruption perception Index 2007,Press Kits,<online>http://www.transparency.org/policy_research/surveys_indices/cpi/2007

(48) Economics Times, "Hit by slowdown, UK property investors look to India",29 May, 2008 <online>
http://economictimes.indiatimes.com/Markets/Real_Estate/Realty_Trends/Hit_by_slowdown_UK_property_investors_look_to_India/articleshow/3081899.cms

(49)Financial Times, "Report says India to grow 8% until 2020", January 24 2007, <online> http://www.ft.com/cms/s/0/6f50980c-abd6-11db-a0ed-0000779e2340.html

(50) Kuvera India, "Why India"<online> http://www.kuvera-india.com/whyindia.aspx

(51)Kuvera India,"News" http://www.kuvera- india.com/readmore.aspx?ID=34

(52)Indian Reality News, "No takers for 2 Plots at BKC Mumbai", March 20, 2008, <online> http://www.indianrealtynews.com/category/property-prices/

(53) Times of India," Property prices in Mumbai to fall by 15%", 13 Jun 2008, <online>
http://timesofindia.indiatimes.com/Cities/Mumbai_property_prices_to_fall_by_15/articleshow/3126889.cms

(54) Hindustan Times, "Real estate prices under pressure", Mumbai, June 12, 2008<online>
http://www.hindustantimes.com/StoryPage/StoryPage.aspx?id=d9cd9016-491e-4b49-b92e-

87654eb5f8ab&MatchID1=4689&TeamID1=4&TeamID2=1&Match
Type1=1&SeriesID1=1182&MatchID2=4699&TeamID3=2&TeamID4=5&MatchTy
pe2=5&SeriesID2=1186&PrimaryID=4689&Headline=Real+estate+prices+under
+pressure

(55) Indian Reality News, "Investors in Delhi NCR having a tough time", March
19, 2008 <online> http://www.indianrealtynews.com/real-estate-
india/investors-in-delhi-ncr-having-a-tough-time.html

(56) Indian Reality News, "DDA Struggling to Find Takers for Hotel Plots", April
2, 2007<online> http://www.indianrealtynews.com/real-estate-
india/delhi/dda-struggling-to-find-takers-for-hotel-plots.html

(57) Economics Times," Reality bites tech hubs in Bangalore, Chennai", 24 Apr,
2008, <online>
http://economictimes.indiatimes.com/News_by_Industry/Realty_bites_tech_h
ubs_in_Bangalore_Chennai/articleshow/2976761.cms

(58) The Times of India," Many top city builders in dire straits," 14 Jun 2008,
<online>
http://timesofindia.indiatimes.com/Cities/Mumbai/Many_top_city_builders_i
n_dire_straits/articleshow/msid-3128002,curpg-2.cms

(59) India PR Wire, "MagicBricks.com survey results on affordable homes; Two-
bedrooms within Rs 5-10 lakh most in demand" 15 April 2008 <online>
http://www.indiaprwire.com/pressrelease/real-estate/200804158772.htm

(60) BBC News, "Merrill Lynch posts $7.8bn loss, "Thursday, 17 January
2008<online> http://news.bbc.co.uk/1/hi/business/7193915.stm

(61) The Hindu, " Multi-crore scam in real estate unearthed", Jul 12, 2007,
<online>
http://www.thehindu.com/2007/07/12/stories/2007071255490300.htm

(62) The Times of India, "Chargesheet against Punjab ex-CM in real estate
scam",13 Dec 2007, <online>
http://timesofindia.indiatimes.com/India/Chargesheet_against_Punjab_ex-
CM_in_real_estate_scam/articleshow/2618435.cms

(63) Rediff, "Only 39.5% Indian graduates employable", May 16, 2008 <online>
http://www.rediff.com/money/2008/may/16job.htm

(64) IBN, "Most B-schools score low in economics test", May 20, 2008,<online> http://www.ibnlive.com/news/most-bschools-score-low-in-economics-test/65620-7.html

(65) The Times of India, "Supreme Court okays quotas in IIMs, IITs",10 Apr 2008,<online> http://timesofindia.indiatimes.com/articleshow/2940232.cms

(66) Economics Times, "Job quota in pvt sector will reverse reforms, says FICCI",23 May, 2008 <online> http://economictimes.indiatimes.com/articleshow/3066907.cms

(67) NDTV, "Hefty pay packets threat to Indian IT cos," May 25, 2008, <online> http://www.ndtvprofit.com/2008/05/25132755/Hefty-pay-packets-threat-to-In.html

(68) Economics Times, "India losing sheen as offshore R & D hub," 20 Feb, 2008, <online> http://economictimes.indiatimes.com/Research_Reports/India_losing_sheen_as_offshore_R__D_hub/articleshow/2797249.cms

(69) Financial Times, "Indian IT outsource companies face tough conditions", April 22 2008 <online> http://www.ft.com/cms/s/0/83b8372e-1097-11dd-b8d6-0000779fd2ac,dwp_uuid=a6dfcf08-9c79-11da-8762-0000779e2340.html

(70) Economics Times,"TCS, Infy, Wipro, Satyam witness sharp slowdown",22 Apr, 2008, <online> http://economictimes.indiatimes.com/Infotech/ITeS/TCS_Infy_Wipro_Satyam_witness_sharp_slowdown/articleshow/2969307.cms

(71) BBC News, "Indian Infosys recruits in the UK",9 October 2007,<online>http://news.bbc.co.uk/1/hi/business/7035297.stm

(72) Rediff, "Indian BPO to offer 800 jobs in Ireland" May 03, 2008,<online> http://www.rediff.com/money/2008/may/03bpo.htm

(73) Hindustan Times,"Wipro opens centre in Malaysia", 21st feb 2008,<online> http://www.hindustantimes.com/StoryPage/StoryPage.aspx?id=19847b18-17b8-4fbb-8777-402c1f53184a&MatchID1=4678&TeamID1=6&TeamID2=3&MatchType1=1&SeriesID1=1179&PrimaryID=4678&Headline=Wipro+opens+centre+in+Malaysia

(74) BBC News, Chennai, India, "Indian IT firms escape rising costs"<online> http://news.bbc.co.uk/1/hi/business/7322802.stm

(75) Rediff, "India no longer top outsourcing destination?", March 05, 2008, <online> http://www.rediff.com/money/2008/mar/05bpo.htm

(76) The Times of India, "Aviva to cut India operations",3 Mar 2008,<online> http://timesofindia.indiatimes.com/articleshow/2832544.cms

(77) The Economics Times, "Rising costs, attrition put 15% of MNC captives in exit mode..."25 Apr, 2008 <online> http://economictimes.indiatimes.com/15_of_MNC_captives_in_exit_mode/arti cleshow/2980334.cms

(78) Hindustan Times, "BPO Meltdown heat: US banks hold meetings to pacify panic-stricken staff", 19th March <online> http://www.hindustantimes.com/StoryPage/StoryPage.aspx?id=6eca8eb3-76c5-4090-995b-13db36260ccf&&Headline=BPO+Meltdown%3a+US+banks+hold+meetings+to+pacify+staff

(79) Economics Times, "Infosys trying new tricks to cut training costs",13 Jun, 2008, <online> http://economictimes.indiatimes.com/Markets/Real_Estate/News_/Infy_tryin g_new_tricks_to_cut_training_costs/articleshow/3126025.cms

(80) The Times of India, "Train delays cause more man-hour losses than strikes"22 Mar 2008, <online> http://timesofindia.indiatimes.com/Train_delays_cause_more_man-hour_losses_than_strikes/articleshow/2888569.cms

(81) The Hindus Business Line," Efficient ports boost GDP growth", Jun 02, 2008,<online> http://www.thehindubusinessline.com/2008/06/02/stories/2008060250300600.htm

(82) DNA India, "Dogs on runways are here to stay," March 29, 2008, <online> http://www.dnaindia.com/report.asp?newsid=1157888

(83) The Hindus, Business, "Poor infrastructure a major hurdle: U.S. CEOs" May04, 2006, <online> http://www.thehindu.com/2006/03/04/stories/2006030405901500.htm

(84) Demographics of India, From Wikipedia, the free encyclopedia < online> http://en.wikipedia.org/wiki/Demographics_of_India

148

(85) The Times of India, 9 farmers commit suicide in Vidarbha
6 Apr 2008, <online>
http://timesofindia.indiatimes.com/9_farmers_commit_suicide_in_Vidarbha/ar
ticleshow/2930933.cms

(86) The Times of India, "2 Amravati farmers commit suicide" 30 Mar 2008
<online>
http://timesofindia.indiatimes.com/2_Amravati_farmers_commit_suicide/artic
leshow/2910793.cms

(87) The Times of India "Farmer suicide in prosperous western UP" 9 May 2007
<online> http://timesofindia.indiatimes.com/articleshow/2020078.cms

(88) The Economics Times, "Retail food prices rise 40% in 4 metros; Delhi worst
hit" 6 Apr, 2008 <online>
http://economictimes.indiatimes.com/Economy/Retail_food_prices_rise_40_in
_metros/articleshow/2930657.cms

(89) IBN LIVE,"In booming India, hunger kills 6,000 kids daily" March 29,2008
<online> http://www.ibnlive.com/news/in-booming-india-hunger-kills-6000-
kids-daily/62220-17.html

(90) The Tribune, Indian at Sixty; "Criminal-politician nexus getting stronger,"
15th August 2007, <online>
http://www.tribuneindia.com/2007/20070815/independence/main6.htm

(91) NDTV, "Govt admits 20 lakh jobs lost in export sector,"March 19,
2008<online> http://www.ndtvprofit.com/2008/03/19174425/Govt-admits-20-
lakh-jobs-lost.html

(92) Doing Business, Economy Ranking, <online>
http://www.doingbusiness.org/economyrankings/

Useful websites

(1)Doing Business

http://www.doingbusiness.org/   (World Bank group)

(2) Federation of Indian Chambers of commerce and Industry (FICCI)

www.ficci.com

(3)National Association of Software and Services Companies (NASSCOM) (Chamber of commerce of the IT-BPO industry in India)

www.nasscom.org

 (4)India Image

http://indiaimage.nic.in

(5)Ministry of Finance

www.finmin.nic.in

(6) Transparency International

http://www.transparency.org/

 (7) The Times of India

 www.timesofindia.indiatimes.com

 (8)The Economics Times

 www.economictimes.indiatimes.com

(9)Business Standard

 www.business-standard.com

(10)Hindu Business Line

 www.thehindubusinessline.com

<u>Our Published Book</u>

Understanding Indian Culture

&

Bridging the Communication Gap

"An inside journey to an Indian mind"

This is a **practical book about bridging the communication gap** between India and the West and understanding Indian culture.

This book will help you to understand what motivates Indians, how they negotiate, where they spend most of their money, what the younger Indian generation wants, etc.

It is based on real life experiences and will help you to understand Indians psychology which will make you more effective while doing business with Indians.

ISBN 978-0-9556882-5-6
Page 100 / Soft Cover / £14.95

For more details

Please visit our website: www.subodhgupta.co.uk

For any query related to bulk purchase please send us your email at:
info@subodhgupta.co.uk

All our books are also available at Amazon.co.uk, Barnes and Nobles

Search Engine Optimization Simplified

"Simplified book on Search Engine Optimization"

The objective of this book is to help you to improve the ranking of your website on all the major search engines like Google, Yahoo and MSN, so that you can increase your sales.

This book contains practical and effective tips to optimise your website.

You can learn how to create search engine friendly pages, choose effective keywords, what search engine likes and especially what it dislike so that you can avoid costly mistakes which can lead to a ban on a website.

This book is ideal for webmasters, university professors, online marketers and entrepreneurs who want to understand Search Engine Optimization in the simplest way.

ISBN 978-0-9556882-8-7
Page 68 / Soft Cover / £8.95

For more details

Please visit our website: www.subodhgupta.co.uk

For any query related to bulk purchase please send us your email at:
info@subodhgupta.co.uk

All our books are also available at Amazon.co.uk, Barnes and Nobles

Training workshops at workplace in London

We provide following workshops for corporate organizations in London.

(1)Understanding Indian Culture and Bridging the Communication gap.

(2)Doing Business in India and Understanding the Pitfalls.

(3)Half day Workshop on Work Life Balance.

(4)Half day workshop on Search Engine Optimization

For more details please contact:

Barbara Tomasik
44(0)7966275913 (London) or info@subodhgupta.co.uk

<u>Our upcoming books:</u>

- **Training – Simplified**

- **Marketing - Simplified**

- **Entrepreneurship - Simplified**

Notes

Notes

www.ingramcontent.com/pod-product-compliance
Ingram Content Group UK Ltd.
Pitfield, Milton Keynes, MK11 3LW, UK
UKHW041324190726
13851UKWH00013B/86